A Gift For:

From:

© 2015 by Katie Farrell.

All rights reserved. No part of this publication may be reproduced, transmitted, or stored in any form or by any means without the prior written permission of the publisher.

Published in 2015 by Hallmark Gift Books, a division of Hallmark Cards, Inc., Kansas City, MO 64141 under license from Thomas Nelson.

Visit us on the Web at Hallmark.com.

Photography by Katie Farrell.

Unless otherwise noted, Scripture quotations are taken from the HOLY BIBLE, NEW INTERNATIONAL VERSION®, NIV®. Copyright © 1973, 1978, 1984, 2011 by Biblica, Inc.® Used by permission of Zondervan. All rights reserved worldwide. www.zondervan.com

Scripture quotations marked NKJV are taken from THE NEW KING JAMES VERSION. © 1982 by Thomas Nelson, Inc. Used by permission. All rights reserved.

Scripture quotations marked NLT are taken from *Holy Bible*, New Living Translation. © 1996. Used by permission of Tyndale House Publishers, Inc., Wheaton, Illinois 60189. All rights reserved.

Scripture quotations marked AMP are taken from THE AMPLIFIED BIBLE: OLD TESTAMENT. ©1962, 1964 by Zondervan (used by permission); and from THE AMPLIFIED BIBLE: NEW TESTAMENT. © 1958 by the Lockman Foundation (used by permission).

Scripture quotations marked ESV are taken The English Standard Version®, © 2001 by Crossway Bibles a division of Good News Publishers.

Scripture quotations marked NASB are taken from NEW AMERICAN STANDARD BIBLE®, © The Lockman Foundation 1960, 1962, 1963, 1968, 1971, 1972, 1973, 1975, 1977, 1995. Used by permission.

ISBN 978-1-59530-788-0

1BOK2231

Made in China

AUG15

Delicious Devotions

Thomas Nelson
Since 1798

NASHVILLE   MEXICO CITY   RIO DE JANEIRO

Feeding Mind, Body, and Soul

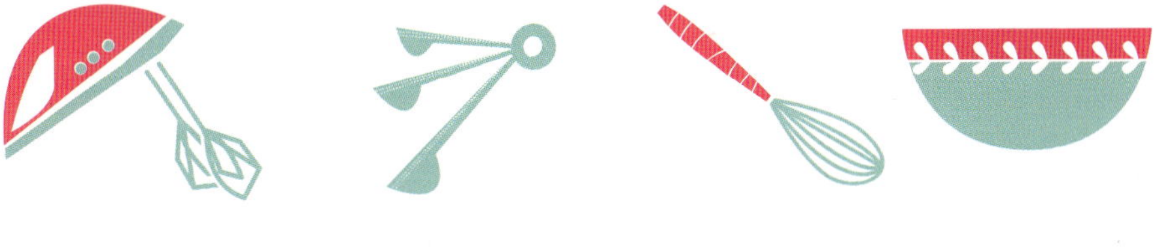

BY KATIE FARRELL

Contents

Introduction **vi**

10 Steps to a Healthier You **vii**

Prayers for Health **ix**

Identity Scriptures **xii**

Devotions **1**

Introduction

Through my Website *Dashing Dish*, I have had the privilege of connecting with women from all different walks of life. After speaking with thousands of women, I found that two things remained consistent—they all desired a transformation of their body image and they wanted advice on improving their health. Whether it was their mental health (relating to depression, eating disorders, or controlling tendencies) or their physical health (stemming from weight-related issues), the question remained the same—*How do I honor my body?*

The reason my heart is moved in such a deep way when it comes to this subject is that I, too, can relate to this question. I have been through every form of disordered eating you can imagine, and I have suffered the mental and physical effects from the years of abuse that I heaped on my own body.

Years later, I can honestly say that I am not who I used to be. In fact, if I try to think back to who I was, it almost feels like a distant dream rather than a memory. I have been transformed from the inside out by renewing my mind with the Word of God!

After finding freedom, encouragement, and balance in my own life, it is truly my greatest heart's desire to help others do the same. I have poured my heart into this devotional, hoping that it will bring life-giving nourishment through the Word of God, as well as practical tools to anyone who picks it up.

I pray that this devotional will inspire you to honor God with your body from the inside out! I will share with you ideas and techniques from my own personal experience of getting in shape and doing it God's way. With healthy recipes, meal planning, workouts, and ministry, it is truly my goal to inspire you to get fit and healthy for life, all while enjoying the journey!

Blessings,
Katie

10 Steps to a Healthier You

Living a healthy lifestyle does not have to be hard work or a drastic change. The best place to start is by making small changes in your everyday life. By making simple swaps and setting small goals, before you know it, these changes will become habits! This list is a handy guide to ten small changes you can make that will help you take little steps toward a healthier you.

1. Get motivated to reach your goals this upcoming year. Find a Bible verse, quote, or picture of yourself when you were in your best shape and place it on your fridge, mirror, or where you can see it. Let this visual reminder inspire and motivate you to press toward your goals!

2. Get moving! Do something active for at least 30 minutes every day. If you have three ten-minute blocks each day, you can fit in a 30-minute exercise. Take a ten-minute walk each day, three times a day, if you don't have time for a traditional workout. It will not only get your blood pumping, which is good for your heart, but it will release feel-good endorphins as well!

3. Often when we think we are hungry, we are actually just thirsty. Make it your goal starting today to drink at least 8 glasses of water each day. To make it easier to get your daily requirement, try adding lemon and stevia to make your water taste like lemonade.

4. Practice speaking life-giving words over yourself and others today. Focus on only speaking positively about your goals for your weight and living a healthier life. Your words are more powerful than you may know. Use them to bless, encourage, and build up those around you!

5. Instead of eating processed snacks that are made with white sugar and flour (such as crackers, chips, and cookies) try swapping them out with whole-grain snacks that have no added sugars. These snacks will help keep you satisfied and are more nourishing for your body.

6. Clean out your pantry and fridge. Throw away (or give away) the processed foods and replace them with nutritious foods. Focus on fruits, vegetables, whole grains, lean proteins, and low-fat dairy. By getting your pantry and fridge stocked with healthy items you can ensure that you and your family are eating well-rounded and healthy meals.

7. Start paying attention to portion sizes. It may help to measure food with measuring cups or a food scale until you become more familiar with proper portion sizes.

8. Focus on cooking at home. Restaurants add a ton of salt, and meals often have "hidden" calories. Limit eating out to once a week or less. When you do go out to eat, look for items on the menu that have lean protein and vegetables, such as a grilled chicken breast with a side of steamed vegetables.

9. Get in the habit of planning ahead when it comes to your workouts. Sit down at the beginning of each week or month and write down at least three workouts per week on your calendar. Once they are planned, treat them like appointments that you can't miss. This will ensure that you don't miss your workouts when your schedule gets busy.

10. Setting goals is the first step toward success in any area of your life. Start setting goals today that will move you toward your health and fitness goals. Begin by writing down at least three short-term and three long-term goals in relation to your health. Ask yourself, how big is the goal? If it can be accomplished in a few weeks, it is short-term. Make the short-term goals something that will move you closer to reaching your long-term goals.

Prayers for Health

The Word of God is alive and powerful. Whatever season of life you may be in or whatever difficulties you may be facing, God's Word has an answer, a promise, and a way out. When we pray according to the promises in God's Word, we are praying in agreement with what God says about us. Nothing has changed my life more than when I began to write down the promises I found in the Bible and put them around my house, car, and wherever I could see them throughout the day.

These are some of the scriptures I have found over the years about taking care of my health and my body and keeping my life well balanced. I have turned these verses into prayers I can pray throughout the day. You can do this with any area of your life. I encourage you to ask the Lord to show you scriptures that He has specifically for you. I pray you are encouraged today by these prayers and that the awesome Word of God reminds you of who you are in Christ and the victory you can have in Him!

God, I thank You that You are for me today. I thank You that You are strengthening me, helping me, and upholding me with Your righteous right hand. —**ROMANS 8:31; ISAIAH 41:10**

Today I make the choice to set aside every burden and the sin I used to be entangled in, and I run with patience the race that is set before me, looking to Jesus, the author and finisher of my faith. —**HEBREWS 12:1-2**

Today I can do all things through Christ who gives me strength. I thank You that through You I can be victorious in everything I do! —**PHILIPPIANS 4:13; 1 CORINTHIANS 15:57**

Thank You, Father, that You have good plans for me regarding my health and for helping me reach and maintain a healthy weight. You have a great future for me, and You have filled me with hope! —JEREMIAH 29:11

I thank You, Lord, that as I submit myself to You today and resist the enemy and his lies, the devil must flee from me in Jesus' name. —JAMES 4:7

Today I make the choice to be self-controlled and alert. I will stay on guard by keeping my eyes fixed on Jesus and staying constant in prayer so I will not fall into temptation. —1 PETER 5:8; MATTHEW 26:41

Today I will take care of my body, for I am God's masterpiece, created in Christ Jesus to do good works, which He has prepared in advance for me to do. —EPHESIANS 2:10

Thank You, Lord, that You will guide me continually today, giving me water when I feel thirsty and restoring my strength when I feel weak. —ISAIAH 58:11

Today I make the choice to treat my body as a gift. It was bought with a price, and I will glorify God in the choices and actions I make when it comes to my body. —1 CORINTHIANS 6:19-20

Instead of indulging my flesh with physical cravings, today I will work up an appetite for God's Word. When I choose to fill up on His Word, He will satisfy me more completely than anything on this earth ever could! —MATTHEW 5:6

Today I will meditate on who God says I am. I will not be conformed to this world, but rather I will choose to renew my mind with the Word of God and be transformed! When I do this, I will be able to discern God's perfect will for my life, my health, and my body. —ROMANS 12:2

Lord, today I will trust in You with all my heart, and I will not lean any longer on my own understanding. I will submit all my ways to You today, and I thank You that, as I do, You will make my paths straight. —PROVERBS 3:5-6

I praise You, Lord, for You are the Father of compassion and the God of all comfort. You comfort me in all my troubles so I can comfort others with the comfort I have received from You. —2 CORINTHIANS 1:3-4

Lord, I thank You that my sinful self was crucified with Christ. I am no longer a slave to sin, and I am free from its power! Therefore, I will not let sin control the way I live. I will not give into sinful desires, but will give myself completely to God. —ROMANS 6:6-12

Today I choose to think on those things that please the Spirit of God. As I live by the Spirit, I experience life and peace in every area of my life! —ROMANS 8:5

Identity Scriptures

One of the most important things we can do for our spiritual health is to discover our true identity in Christ and see ourselves as Jesus sees us. One way we can do this is by believing and speaking out the truth of what God says about us in His Word. These scriptures can be used to declare and renew your mind to recognize who you are in Christ. As you begin to learn your identity in Him, you will see a transformation take place in your spirit, mind, and body.

I am adopted as God's child.
—**EPHESIANS 1:5**

I am confident that God will perfect the work He has begun in me.
—**PHILIPPIANS 1:6**

I have not been given a spirit of fear, but of power, love, and self-discipline. —**2 TIMOTHY 1:7**

I am fearfully and wonderfully made. —**PSALM 139:14**

I was chosen before the creation of the world. —**EPHESIANS 1:4, 11**

I am holy and blameless.
—**EPHESIANS 1:4**

I am forgiven. —**EPHESIANS 1:7; COLOSSIANS 1:14**

I have purpose.
—**EPHESIANS 1:9; 3:11**

I am God's workmanship.
—**EPHESIANS 2:10**

I have peace. —**EPHESIANS 2:14**

I am secure. —**EPHESIANS 2:20**

I am a holy temple. —**EPHESIANS 2:21; 1 CORINTHIANS 6:19**

I am a dwelling for the Holy Spirit.
—**EPHESIANS 2:22**

God's power works through me.
—**EPHESIANS 3:7**

I can approach God with confidence. —**EPHESIANS 3:12**

I can bring glory to God.
—**1 CORINTHIANS 10:31**

I have been called.
—**EPHESIANS 4:1; 2 TIMOTHY 1:9**

I can be kind and compassionate to others. —**EPHESIANS 4:32**

I can forgive others.
—**EPHESIANS 4:32**

I am a light to others.
—**EPHESIANS 5:8-9**

I am not alone. —**HEBREWS 13:5**

I possess the mind of Christ.
—**1 CORINTHIANS 2:16**

I am victorious. —**1 JOHN 5:4**

My heart and mind are protected with God's peace.
—**PHILIPPIANS 4:7**

I am chosen and dearly loved.
—**COLOSSIANS 3:12**

I am loved. —**JOHN 3:16**

I am a new creation.
—**2 CORINTHIANS 5:17**

1

The First Day of the Rest of Your Life

If you confess with your mouth the Lord Jesus and believe in your heart that God has raised Him from the dead, you will be saved.
—ROMANS 10:9 NKJV

Creating a healthy mind and body starts with nurturing your relationship with God. He designed each of us to have a special relationship with Him. He created man and woman to commune with Him. Adam and Eve enjoyed a flawless existence with God in the garden. But when Adam and Eve sinned against God, all of that changed. Man's perfect nature was now imperfect, and people were separated from God by sin.

In the Old Testament, the people of that time had to offer sacrifices for their sins in order to protect themselves from God's wrath. But then everything changed again—God sent His Son, Jesus, so that we could *all* be saved from sin. In the New Testament there is a new covenant, or promise based on what Jesus came to earth to do for us—to be the ultimate sacrifice for our sins. Instead of animal blood repeatedly being shed to atone for sins, Jesus shed His blood for all our past, present, and future sins. Jesus came to save all of humankind. It is His gift to us; but it is up to us to accept this gift.

Romans 10:9 says when you confess Jesus as Lord and believe this truth in your heart, you are saved. When you accept Jesus as Lord of your life, you are no longer separated from Him—you are born again! You will spend eternity (life after death) in heaven with the Lord. The good news is that the blessings of walking with the Lord aren't just for eternity; they are for life on earth as well. In addition to eternal salvation and forgiveness of sins, a relationship with Jesus gives us wisdom, comfort, purpose, and so much more! Spiritual health is the foundation for a healthy body. When I began to strengthen my relationship with Jesus, it was then that I was able to improve my physical health and find balance.

Lord, I thank You for sending Your Son, Jesus, to die for my sins and to allow me to have a relationship with my Creator. Jesus, I thank You that You no longer remember my sins. I believe that everything I was is now crucified on the cross with You, and I now have a new nature in Christ. Lord, give me strength to follow the path You designed for me. I believe that You will guide me and change me from the inside out. Today is the first day of the rest of my life! In Jesus' name, amen.

Dash of Inspiration

I remember one of the first times I allowed my relationship with God to affect my physical health. God began to teach me that one of the greatest tools He gave me is the ability to listen to my body. This means eating until you are satisfied—not stuffed, but satisfied. This has helped me live a healthier lifestyle both physically and mentally, and it has helped me develop a healthy, balanced relationship with food. Rather than eating everything that is on my plate, or having the mentality that some foods are off limits, I try to enjoy everything in moderation. I take a few bites, put my fork down, and really pay attention to my body. When I feel like my stomach is satisfied, I stop. This process took a period of learning, but eventually I became in tune with my body.

sugar · paper
LOS ANGELES

BREAKFAST   LUNCH   DINNER

RECIPE

2

How Do You See Yourself?

For as [a man] thinks in his heart, so is he.
—PROVERBS 23:7 NKJV

This verse is very clear: what we think about ourselves too often becomes a self-fulfilling prophecy. If we choose to think about who we are in the flesh—who we are naturally, who we are without Jesus—we will see shortcomings and failure. If we choose to focus on these limitations, then it won't take long before we find our lives heading in that unwanted direction.

Ever since I was in elementary school, I believed that I wasn't good at sports. I would tell people right away that I couldn't catch a ball or throw one for the life of me. That's how I saw myself for over twenty years! Now that I'm approaching thirty, I'm finally realizing that this is not true at all. God tells me that in Him I can do all things. All these years I was focusing on my shortcomings and saw myself as weak and unable rather than believing the strengths within me.

If, however, we choose to think about who we are in Christ—which is who we truly are—then we will begin to believe in our hearts that we are loved, valuable, forgiven, and cherished. As we read God's Word and see in black and white the truths about who God says we are, we have an opportunity to choose to *believe* those statements. And if we do, we will find ourselves becoming all that He says we are and all that He says we can be.

What lies do you need to stop telling yourself today? How can you grab hold of God's truth about your identity in Him?

Jesus, please show me in Your Word who I truly am in Your eyes and who You have created me to be. Help me focus on who You say I am and what You say I am capable of accomplishing through You. Lord, I want to live the life that You have designed for me, and by Your grace and in Your power, fulfill Your plans for me. In Jesus' name, amen.

3

Knowing Who We Are

See what great love the Father has lavished on us, that we should be called children of God! And that is what we are!
—1 JOHN 3:1

I distinctly remember my first day of seventh grade. I had just moved to a very small town, which meant that everyone recognized me as being new. The thing I recall the most on that first day was trying to find a group of people I could sit with at lunch. As I aimlessly wandered through the lunch room, I remember scanning over the different types of groups and cliques, trying to find a place where I would belong, but feeling very left out and alone. It was around that time that Satan started to get me to believe lies about myself. I started to feel unsure about my appearance, which eventually led to lies that had me questioning who God created me to be.

From the very beginning, Satan has been in the business of making us question our identity. We can see one example of this when he tempted Jesus in the wilderness. Two out of his three temptations began with the words, "If you are the Son of God" (Luke 4:3, 9), which makes it very clear that the attack was aimed at Jesus' identity. Satan was trying to get Jesus to question who He was at the very core.

And two thousand years later, Satan is still trying his old tricks, so we can be sure that he will use the very same tactics to tempt us. Whether he lies to us personally, or whether he uses others to attack us, telling us that we will never be good enough, we need to be aware of his schemes.

Yes, he may use different ways to get there, but we need to know that one of Satan's methods of attack is to get us to question the core of our identity. If he can get us doubting whether we are actually children of God, then he has essentially stripped us of the power and authority we have over him as God's children. Satan wants nothing more than for us to lose our identity as children of God, for then we would wander like sheep without a Shepherd.

The good news is we can easily defeat Satan's lies by following Jesus' example in the wilderness. God has given us all the same enemy-defeating weapon that Jesus used to overcome Satan's schemes—His Word. So the next time the enemy comes at you with lies, trying to rob you of your identity, stand against him with the Word, with prayer, and with praise!

We can stand strong against Satan's lies by walking closely with God, day by day, moment by moment. When we spend time, for instance, renewing our minds with the Word of God during quiet time, prayer, and journaling, the Lord will build our confidence about who we are in Him. You *are* a child of God!

Lord, thank You for calling me Your child. What an honor to approach You as Father! Help me be aware when the enemy attacks, calling into question my identity as Your daughter. Enable me to stand against his lies with the powerful weapon of Your truth. I thank You that *nothing* can separate me from Your love. In Jesus' name, amen.

4

True Beauty

Do not let your adorning be external—the braiding of hair and the putting on of gold jewelry, or the clothing you wear—but let your adorning be the hidden person of the heart with the imperishable beauty of a gentle and quiet spirit, which in God's sight is very precious.
—1 PETER 3:3-4 ESV

We are so used to seeing ourselves in a mirror. By looking in a mirror we can see if our hair looks messy or if our makeup looks just right. We have learned to trust what the mirror tells us. We are so used to trusting it that often we find ourselves giving it the right to tell us if we are beautiful. A mirror is not a reliable voice! The Word of God, however, is a reliable mirror (James 1:23), and it tells us our *true* identity.

Although we can often feel better about ourselves by getting dressed up and fixing our hair, those externals do not define beauty, and they do not define us. The Word of God does.

When we look in a mirror of glass and find flaws, God reminds us that in His true mirror, "You are altogether beautiful, my love; there is no flaw in you" (Song of Solomon 4:7 ESV). Hear this praise to our Creator: "You formed my inward parts;

You covered me in my mother's womb. I will praise You, for I am fearfully and wonderfully made" (Psalm 139:13–14, NKJV).

If you find yourself believing what the glass mirror tells you about yourself and your value, run to the mirror that is true and matters most: God's Word, which will always reveal your true beauty.

> **Lord, help me remember** that whatever the mirror shows is not what You find most beautiful about me. You who formed me before I was born look at my inward parts, and You love me. So help me not to judge myself by the world's standards, but to find my identity and worth in Your love. In Jesus' name, amen.

Cinnamon Roll No-Bake Breakfast Cookies

INGREDIENTS:
½ cup creamy peanut butter (or nut butter of choice)
2½ tbs low-sugar maple syrup or honey
¾ cup old-fashioned oats (not quick oats)
¼ cup protein powder (or additional oats, or almond/oat flour)
¼ cup baking stevia (or ½ cup sweetener that measures like sugar)
Pinch salt
½ tsp cinnamon

METHOD:
1. In a small microwavable bowl, combine the peanut butter and syrup or honey. Microwave for about 20 to 30 seconds (or until the peanut butter is just melted), then stir until combined. Stir in the oats, protein powder, stevia, salt, and cinnamon, mixing until everything is completely combined.
2. Roll the dough into 7 even-sized balls, and flatten each ball slightly with your hands, molding it into a cookie shape. Place each cookie on a piece of parchment paper or foil lightly sprayed with cooking spray to prevent sticking. Enjoy cookies right away, or place them in a covered container in your fridge for up to 1 week, or in your freezer for up to 3 months.

SERVINGS: 7 (1 cookie per serving)

5

Freedom in Forgiveness

Bear with each other and forgive one another if any of you has a grievance against someone. Forgive as the Lord forgave you.
—COLOSSIANS 3:13

Not too long ago I was faced with an offense that, when not dealt with, grew larger within me. By that evening, the itty-bitty offense soon turned into resentment, anger, and bitterness. Not dealing with it from the beginning didn't affect the other person; it was solely affecting me.

Relationships can be the greatest joy in life, and, at the same time, they can be incredibly damaging. Maybe things have been done to you or said about you that seem unforgivable. Or you may want to forgive, but feel trapped by the hurt and pain still gnawing at your heart. Often we find ourselves in self-protection mode when we have been hurt. We put up walls and shut people out. We can't get hurt if we never let anyone in! But this is not God's plan for us: He calls us to forgive.

One of the most important things to realize is that forgiveness is not a feeling; it is an obedient response to God's commandment to forgive. Forgiveness also isn't excusing someone for bad behavior. When you forgive, you aren't allowing that person to get away with what he or she has done. Rather you are deciding not to take your own vengeance—that's God's department (Roman's 12:19). Forgiveness is for *you*. It sets *you* free. When you hold on to the hurt and pain of your past, you keep yourself bound to the past.

True freedom comes when we understand who Jesus is and how He came to forgive His followers of past, present, and future sins. We see in the Bible that Jesus didn't just forgive the people of their sins; He also forgave them for sinning against Him, for sinning against the Lord Himself. Anytime we are tempted to hold on to what someone has done to us, we need to remember how Jesus was beaten, cursed, and crucified. People wrongly accused Him to His face. Despite the pain of those words and the physical pain of the crucifixion, Jesus still prayed, "Father, forgive them, for they do not know what they are doing" (Luke 23:34).

Forgiveness goes beyond what our flesh tells us to do—and beyond what our flesh is even able to do. We must remain mindful of what our Father has forgiven us and forgive one another by faith, in obedience, and in God's power.

Are you struggling to forgive someone? Pray the prayer below and ask for God's help.

> **Lord, help me forgive** _____ for _____.
> Help me remember that You have forgiven and love that person just as You have forgiven and love me. Help me forgive this person. Please take away my hurt, anger, and bitterness and bring healing and restoration. In Jesus' name, amen.

6

Don't Give Up!

Let us not become weary in doing good, for at the proper time we will reap a harvest if we do not give up.

—GALATIANS 6:9

God has a plan full of the kind of freedom, joy, and peace that this world could never give. However, in this fast-paced society, this plan often takes longer to unfold than most of us would like. This is where patience and endurance come in! Patience is such a vital part of attaining the plan God has for us. Often we can be the reason for the delay in seeing His plan. If we have established bad habits, it can take time for us to learn to allow God to renew our minds and change our actions.

Before a fitness routine becomes a fixed part of your day, for example, it may take a good amount of time and discipline to wake up early to work out. In fact, at first you will probably find it painful to get rid of some of your old habits and make better choices. The Bible even tells us this will be the case: "No discipline is enjoyable while it is happening—it's painful! But afterward there will be a peaceful harvest of right living for those who are trained in this way" (Hebrews 12:11 NLT). If we endure the temporary pain that comes with disciplining ourselves and if we continue to make the right choices, we can be sure that a harvest awaits us that will produce a great peace within.

The next time you are tempted to give up on something, remind yourself of this truth. If you keep doing the good things God has set before you, then you will reap a wonderful harvest.

> **Lord, when I am feeling discouraged,** please help me keep doing the good things you set before me with patient endurance. I know that if I don't give up, then I will receive the wonderful things You have planned for me. Help me be renewed with Your strength and patience today. In Jesus' name, amen.

15-Minute Skinny Shrimp Fried Rice

INGREDIENTS:

2 cups whole grain rice, uncooked

2 large eggs, slightly beaten

½ medium onion, finely diced

1 tbs garlic, minced (or ½ tsp garlic powder)

¾ cup frozen carrots, diced

¾ cup frozen peas

12 oz frozen shrimp (medium-sized, cooked, peeled, deveined, tail-on shrimp)

2 green onions, diced

3 to 4 tbs low-sodium soy sauce

METHOD:
1. Prepare the rice according to package directions, and set aside.
2. Meanwhile, spray a large nonstick skillet with nonstick cooking spray and heat over medium heat. Add in the eggs and cook for a few minutes, until they are are cooked through. Use a spatula to break the eggs apart into small pieces. Remove from the pan and set aside.
3. Re-spray the pan with cooking spray. Add in the diced onion and ¼ cup water and cook for a few minutes, until the onions are tender and translucent. Add garlic and sauté for 1 to 2 minutes longer, or until the onions and garlic are starting to get lightly golden brown.
4. Add carrots and peas. Toss in shrimp and stir-fry for a few minutes, or until the shrimp are warmed through and the veggies are just starting to get tender.
5. To the pan, add in cooked rice and green onions. Add soy sauce to the pan. Stir to incorporate. Add the cooked scrambled egg. Stir again to incorporate. When everything is heated through, remove the fried rice from heat and serve warm.

SERVINGS: 4 Servings (about 3 ounces meat and 1 cup rice and vegetables per serving)

7

Dealing with Anxiety

Search me, O God, and know my heart;
> test me and know my anxious thoughts.
Point out anything in me that offends you,
> and lead me along the path of everlasting life.

—PSALM 139:23-24 NLT

No matter where we go or what we do—even if it means we have chosen the wrong path or tried to hide from God—He is with us. We can't do anything that would cause Him to stop thinking about and caring for us! But when we have anxious thoughts about an aspect of life, it shows that we aren't trusting God to take care of us. I personally experienced a lot of anxiety when I was trying to decide my future career path. I went to school to be a nurse, but after only two years of working in a hospital, I felt the Lord calling me in a different direction. This is just one of many times when I have been tempted to be anxious about what the future held.

When we worry about things such as relationships, circumstances, or the future, it means we are depending on ourselves rather than on God, which can eventually steer us off the path God has for us.

If you can relate to these feelings of anxiousness, I would encourage you to ask God to search your heart and reveal to you where these sources of anxiety are coming from. Then make the decision to entrust these areas and everything in your life to Him, and He will show you the best path to take!

Lord, how amazing that You think about me and have a plan for me already laid out (Jeremiah 29:11)! Please forgive me for being anxious and trying to figure things out on my own. And please show me in what ways I am not trusting in You. In Jesus' name, amen!

Dash of Inspiration

I remember being in nursing school and being so busy at times that I felt like I could barely think about my health, but I always knew that it was important to live a healthy lifestyle in order to feel my best and keep stress at bay. One of the greatest things that I did during this time was learn to plan ahead. Taking about an hour every Sunday night allowed me to prepare healthy meals and snacks and to plan my workout schedule for that week. I found that having things like my no-bake cinnamon roll cookies on hand really helped me stay on top of eating healthy despite my busy morning schedule. Even if I didn't have time to fit in a workout, I would do my best to take a 20-minute walk on my lunch break, which helped me release stress and gave me more energy for the rest of the day.

8

The Power of God's Word

My son, pay attention to what I say;
    turn your ear to my words.
Do not let them out of your sight,
    keep them within your heart;
for they are life to those who find them
    and health to one's whole body.

—PROVERBS 4:20–22

I have been through every form of disordered eating you can imagine, as well as suffered the mental and physical effects from the years of abuse that I did to my own body. Over the years I sought professional help from medical doctors and counselors, and although I may have found some temporary relief or hope, it was only a matter of time before I found myself slipping back into old patterns and habits. It wasn't until I woke up one day and made the decision that I was going to look for freedom, healing, and restoration in the One who created me that I found peace. I figured, if God created the universe, then He surely could heal and mend my mind and my body!

When I began my search for true transformation, I remember God leading me to the fourth chapter of Proverbs. It was there that God revealed to me that I could find health for my mind, body, and emotions in His Word. But I also knew I had a part to play in receiving my healing in this area. In order to see the truth of this promise from Proverbs 4 fulfilled in my life, I recognized that I must also observe the first part of this passage, which meant keeping God's Word constantly before my eyes and in my heart.

One practical way that you can keep God's Word in front of your eyes is by writing scriptures on notecards or sticky notes and putting them wherever you will see them. Seeing God's Word throughout the day like this will play a crucial role in your efforts to renew your mind; you can combat the lies of this world with the truth of God's Word.

As the truth of what you believe becomes more and more rooted in your heart, you will find it easier to keep that truth in the forefront of your mind. Before too long, you'll begin to believe what God says about you more than what your circumstances may be trying to tell you. When you keep your eyes on God's Word, you will begin to walk in the fullness of all that God has provided.

Thank You, Lord, for Your Word. Help me keep Your truth about Your love for me before my eyes and within my heart. As I keep Your Word before me, root its truths deep in my heart and enable them to produce fruit in my life. In Jesus' name, amen.

9

What Are You Thinking About?

Set your minds and keep them set on what is above (the higher things), not on the things that are on the earth.
—COLOSSIANS 3:2 AMP

Have you ever stopped for a moment to think about the kinds of thoughts that are running through your head? Many of us are passive in our thinking; we allow thoughts to come and go without actually reflecting on what we are thinking about. The Bible tells us to set our minds—and to keep them set—on what is above, on God. And we need to be told to set and keep our thoughts focused on God, because it doesn't happen naturally. We must *actively* choose to set our thoughts on God and His truth every day and throughout each day.

If we don't actively choose where we direct our thoughts, our thinking can fall into a pattern of wrong thoughts that can steal our peace, joy, and strength. But choosing to think, for instance, about what God says in His Word will help us make right choices regardless of what is going on all around us. And by making those right choices, God can use us to impact the world around us in a positive and powerful way.

One thing that helps me keep my mind set on things above is to spend time with God every day. I love to find a comfy and quiet place in my house and sit down with my Bible. As I read, I love to write down verses that apply to what I am going through in that season of my life.

I also love to write scriptures out on sticky notes and keep them where I can see them to help me stay focused on the truth of the Word. It takes time, effort, and consistency to keep our minds set on the things of God, but one thing is for sure: it will always be worth the effort!

> **Lord, I choose this day** to set my mind on You rather than focusing on situations around me. Help me recognize when my thoughts start drifting toward things of this world, and help me stay focused on You and Your Word so I can stay on Your narrow and good path. In Jesus' name, amen.

10

Laying Your Burdens Down

Give your burdens to the Lord,
and he will take care of you.
—PSALM 55:22 NLT

When we give a burden we've been carrying to God, we are trusting Him to keep His promise and to take care of it. If we have decided to pray about something, then we must also choose to give that thing over to the Lord. If, however, we find ourselves still worrying about that situation, we have probably tried to take it back and deal with it on our own. When we recognize that, we can release that burden to the Lord once again.

I remember when my husband and I first got married. I didn't have a job at that time, and we had to rely solely on my husband's income to provide for us. I remember feeling anxious about money, no matter how much my husband tried to reassure me that we were going to be okay. I remember sitting out on our apartment balcony and it finally hit me: I was being anxious and worrying about something that God had promised I didn't have to worry about. It was that day when I released my worry to the Lord.

That releasing is so much easier when we remember that God has promised to take care of us, guide us, and provide for us. If we choose to focus on these promises, releasing our cares—all of them, once and for all—becomes possible. If we find ourselves worrying about something again, then we can choose to stop those anxious thoughts right in their tracks by saying, "No, I refuse to worry about this thing anymore because God is taking care of it!" Our heavenly Father promises that when we do this—when we put our trust in Him, rather than worrying—His peace that passes all understanding will flood our minds (Philippians 4:7).

Lord, You invite me to cast my cares on You, so right now I give You these burdens: _____. If I start to worry again, I pray that Your Holy Spirit will help me stop and choose to focus on You. And I thank You for the perfect peace I know You'll grant. In Jesus' name, amen.

Healthy Snacks

11

Guard Your Heart

Guard your heart above all else,
for it determines the course of your life.
—PROVERBS 4:23 NLT

Proverbs 4:23 is both instruction and explanation. God first instructs us to guard our hearts. Then He explains why it is so important: because whatever is in our hearts will "determine the course" of our lives. In other words, whatever we put into our hearts will impact our lives in one way or another. That is why it is so important to make careful choices about what we let come into our eyes and ears, because they are the gateway to our hearts (Matthew 6:22).

But God doesn't mean we need to live isolated from this world, tucked away so that we don't have to worry about encountering any negative input, but we do need to think twice about what we watch, read, and listen to if we want to live in a way that honors and glorifies God. Paul offered us this very practical advice for guarding our hearts: "Whatever is true, whatever is noble, whatever is right, whatever is pure, whatever is lovely, whatever is admirable—if anything is excellent or praiseworthy—think about such things" (Philippians 4:8). Is there an area in your life where you can begin to guard your heart more carefully? If so, I would encourage you to submit that to the Lord today.

Lord, please help me guard my heart from everything in this world that would pull me away from You, and fill it with praiseworthy thoughts that glorify You. And I ask You, Lord, to keep me on the course of life that You have planned for me. In Jesus' name, amen.

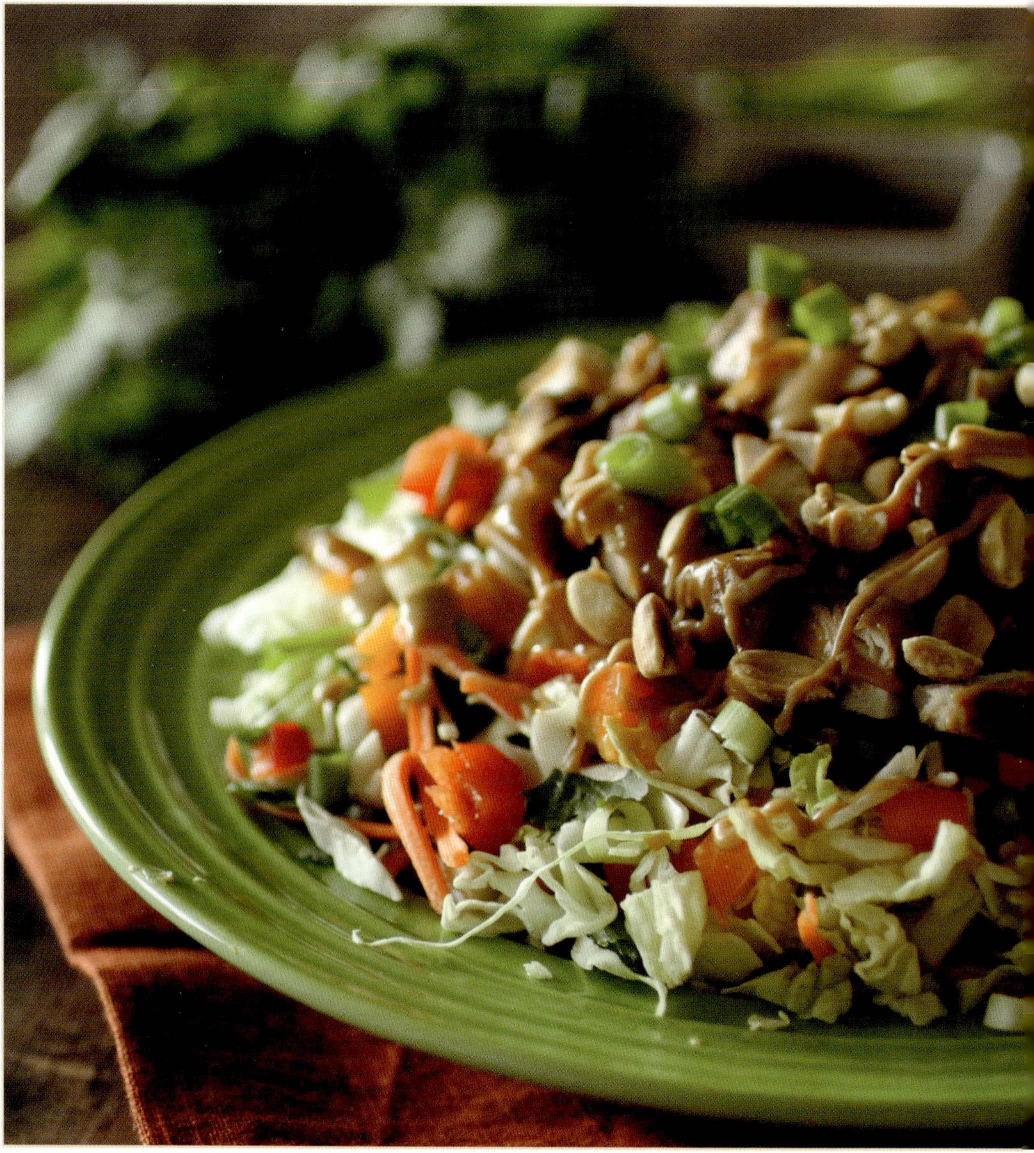

Thai Chicken Salad

INGREDIENTS:

For the Salad:

6 cups pre-cut shredded cabbage mix

1½ cups cooked and shredded chicken breast

2 green onions, thinly sliced

¼ cup chopped cilantro (or small handful)

1 small red bell pepper, finely diced

1 small orange bell pepper, finely diced

Optional: chopped peanuts or almonds for topping

For the Dressing:

¼ cup peanut butter or peanut flour

2 tbs soy sauce

2 tbs rice wine vinegar

1 tbs lime juice

1 tbs honey or sweetener (or to taste)

⅛ tsp dried powdered ginger

pinch of salt and pepper

METHOD:
1. To make the salad: Place cabbage in a large bowl and add the chicken, green onions, cilantro, and bell peppers. Toss to combine.
2. To make the dressing: Microwave peanut butter for 20 to 30 seconds, or until it is just melted. (If you are using peanut flour, simply mix enough of it with water until it is watery enough to resemble melted peanut butter.) Whisk together peanut butter, soy sauce, vinegar, lime juice, honey or sweetener, ginger, salt, and pepper in a small bowl until everything is combined. Refrigerate until ready to serve.
3. When you are ready to enjoy your salad, pour the dressing on top of the salad and gently toss to combine. Divide salad into 2 servings and top with peanuts or almonds if you desire. Enjoy!

SERVINGS: 2

12

Resist and Win

> When the devil had finished all this tempting,
> he left him until an opportune time.
> —LUKE 4:13

Maybe you remember the scene shortly after Jesus was baptized. The Spirit led Jesus into the desert where He would fast for forty days and then be tested by Satan. In an attempt to find in Jesus an area of weakness and vulnerability, Satan presented Him with various temptations. But Jesus stood strong, resisted every temptation, and defeated the enemy.

In addition to being a great example of how to handle temptation (Jesus quoted the Word of God in response to Satan), this scene also gives us a promise we can cling to: when we resist the devil's temptations as Jesus did, he must leave us as well. The Bible teaches that three types of temptation will come against us: the lust of the flesh, the lust of the eyes, and the pride of life (1 John 2:16). When we remember that whatever Satan is fighting us with is temporary, we will find the strength needed to endure the fight against him. We can also take great assurance in knowing that when we resist the devil, God is on our side. He will "provide a way out" (1 Corinthians 10:13).

When I was renewing my mind in the area of eating disorders, Satan would try to tempt me to go back to my former way of life. I would find old thoughts creeping in, tempting me to old habits. However, I recognized those thoughts as the enemy trying to tempt me, and therefore did not give them any of my attention. I also asked the Lord for strength to resist these lies, knowing that He is faithful to provide a way out of every temptation that we face.

Satan would like us to think that he is tougher than he really is. One of his greatest weapons is intimidation, but if you are a child of God, "the one who is in you is greater than the one who is in the world" (1 John 4:4). The devil roams around like a lion seeking to devour those who don't know Christ as their Savior (1 Peter 5:8). When we are being tempted, we must realize that God gives us not only the strength to resist, but He also provides a way out. When we stand strong in the Lord and in the truths of His Word, the devil must leave.

Lord God, I thank You for Your written Word and the powerful name of Jesus that enables me to stand strong against the enemy and his temptations! I thank You, Lord, that You provide me with both a way out of temptation and the strength to resist the devil. In Jesus' name, amen.

13

Faith with Action

You see that [Abraham's] faith and his actions were working together, and his faith was made complete by what he did.
—JAMES 2:22

If you have ever prayed and asked God to change a situation in your life, there's a good chance that His answer required action on your part! Often we ask God to solve a certain problem or give us wisdom about a particular topic, but many times we fail to follow through with the actions that He wants *us* to take.

The area of our health gives us a powerful example. When we ask God to help us reach a healthy weight or to have more energy, He will very likely show us that we need to be more active and choose a more nutritious diet—and that may not be what we want to hear! After all, it would be easier for us if God just solved the problem for us. Changing our comfortable behaviors and our long-held habits can be very difficult and even uncomfortable.

But if we want to effectively represent the Lord, we need our actions to reflect our faith. In this example, we can definitely ask the Lord for the faith and wisdom we need to change our unhealthy habits, but we can't stop at that. If we want to experience the change that we are praying for, we must act according to what God expects from us. When our faith that God will guide and provide is supported by our actions in response to His guidance, we will get results.

This principle applies to many different areas of life. So the next time we go to the Lord for answers, we should not only look to Him for wisdom, but we should also be ready to act as He directs, according to His plan to bring about the change we request. Sometimes God gives us a key role to play—specific actions to take—to bring about His answer to our prayers!

Lord, I ask You to give me wisdom for this area of my life: _____. Thank You for giving me faith and strength to take action as You direct. Help me take the action You specify and cooperate with You as You lead me. And thank You that the faith You have blessed me with will be "made complete" when I back it with actions. In Jesus' name, amen.

14

Reflect on God's Goodness

Praise the Lord, my soul;
    all my inmost being, praise his holy name.
Praise the Lord, my soul,
    and forget not all his benefits—
who forgives all your sins
    and heals all your diseases,
who redeems your life from the pit
    and crowns you with love and compassion,
who satisfies your desires with good things
    so that your youth is renewed like the eagle's.

—PSALM 103:1-5

I don't know about you, but when I'm going through a hard time, the first thing affected is my soul—my mind, will, and emotions. I know that emotions are fickle; they are certainly not something we should live by. I also know that the joy and peace that the Lord gives go much deeper than the emotional highs and lows that come with changing circumstances. Despite knowing all these things as truth, we can still find it difficult to overcome the reality of our sinking emotions, can't we?

One of the most effective ways to overcome negative emotions is by taking a moment to praise the Lord and remind ourselves of how good He is to us. We all have so much to praise Him for. And even if we can't think of something specific, we surely can thank Him for giving us His one and only Son, Jesus, to die for us so we could be washed clean of our sins and have a relationship with the holy God, both now and for eternity! That is reason enough to praise God!

If you find yourself in a challenging season of life, or if you are simply having a hard day, I encourage you to take a moment to reflect on God's goodness. Remind yourself of the good things He has done in your life and that His faithfulness to you and His love for you will never change!

Lord, today I choose to reflect on Your goodness and all the good things You have done in my life. Thank You for Your faithfulness and that Your great love for me will never change. In Jesus' name, amen!

Raspberry Chocolate Chip Muffins

INGREDIENTS:

1¼ cups oat flour (or 1½ cups old-fashioned oats ground into a flour)

¼ cup vanilla protein powder

½ cup baking stevia (or 1 cup sweetener that measures like sugar)

1 tsp baking powder

½ tsp baking soda

½ tsp salt

½ cup plain low-fat Greek yogurt or unsweetened applesauce

1 large egg

1 large egg white

¾ cup fresh raspberries

3 tbs chocolate chips

METHOD:
1. Preheat your oven to 350 degrees. Line 10 muffin tins with silicone or foil muffin liners (to help prevent sticking), and spray with cooking spray.
2. In a medium bowl, mix together oat flour, protein powder, stevia, baking powder, baking soda, salt, yogurt, egg, and egg white. Gently fold the berries and chips into the batter. Divide batter evenly among muffin cups. Bake for 20 to 25 minutes, or until a toothpick comes out clean.

SERVINGS: 10 (1 muffin per serving)

41

15

The Word of Your Testimony

They triumphed over him
> by the blood of the Lamb
> and by the word of their testimony.

—REVELATION 12:11

We have all experienced difficult trials in our lives, some so crushing that we wondered if we would ever see the other side. Those trials may have passed and we may have overcome, yet we still feel wounded, beaten up, and bruised from that weary time. Talking about those trials may be difficult.

God's Word is clear that Satan comes to steal, kill, and destroy (John 10:10). He wants nothing more than to defeat Christians. He lies, threatens, accuses, and intimidates in order to crush believers. Yet as Revelation 12:11 teaches, telling our story—sharing "the word of [our] testimony"—is one way we triumph over our enemy.

Perhaps you don't feel like you have a real testimony to share. Remember that Satan will lie to us, and try to get us to become cowards and to strip us of the identity that Jesus came to give us. The good news is that Jesus has given us powerful weapons to fight these lies of the enemy and triumph over Satan by the "word of

[our] testimony." Your testimony is speaking about what you overcame through Christ and what He has done in your life since that moment you accepted Him as Savior. Many believers are timid about sharing their story because they think either their testimony isn't powerful enough, or they haven't arrived at the point where they should be sharing it with others. Neither of those is true!

First of all, acknowledge that your testimony won't be like anyone else's—and that is what makes it worth sharing! Maybe you grew up in a Christian home and lived a faithful life from early on. That is a testimony. Perhaps you have just recently come to know Christ and are learning to walk out of bondage or addiction. That is a powerful story worth sharing with others! Satan lies to us, telling us that we should feel ashamed of our past or that our transformation isn't great enough to share. Satan wants to keep us silent! But anytime believers open their mouths to share what God has done in their lives—no matter how big or small—they are taking hold of a weapon, taking a stand against Satan, and using what the Lord has done in their lives to transform the lives of others for Him.

What stories can you share today? How might your victories demonstrate the Lord's grace and power to the people around you?

> **Lord, I thank You** for the wonderful things You have done in my life, for the truth of my testimony which You have given me to tell. Please help me be bold as I share my testimony. For I know that it will not only encourage others, but it will also give me power to defeat the enemy in my own life. In Jesus' name, amen.

16

Emotional Eating

"Come, all you who are thirsty,
    come to the waters;
and you who have no money,
    come, buy and eat!
Come, buy wine and milk
    without money and without cost.
Why spend money on what is not bread,
    and your labor on what does not satisfy?
Listen, listen to me, and eat what is good,
    and you will delight in the richest of fare."

—ISAIAH 55:1-2

It is not uncommon for people to turn to food when emotions run high. Whether we are experiencing sadness, stress, loneliness, or even celebratory excitement, we can often find ourselves in the kitchen. This emotional eating—eating prompted by emotions rather than physical hunger—usually involves foods that aren't good for our bodies, as well as excessive amounts of that less-than-healthy food.

So what steps do we take to stop running to food? Jesus called Himself "the bread of life" (John 6:35), and He taught that He gives us "living water" (John 4:10). In other words, we have all been created with a void that can be filled only by Him. We can try filling it with things of this world, such as food, but we will never feel satisfied. That being the case, when we find ourselves dealing with intense emotions—usually low, but sometimes high—we need to learn to run to the Word, which is the only thing that will satisfy our true hunger.

Again, emotional eating isn't about the food; it's about the emotions we are feeling in the moment. God's Word has all the answers to all our problems. So when we have emotional hunger pangs, let's go to Jesus and cast our cares upon Him, find wisdom for our problems, or simply praise Him for His defeat of sin and His love for us. Only in Jesus will you find true satisfaction and nourishment for your soul.

Lord, I thank You—You who are the bread of life and the living water—that You satisfy my soul. The next time I'm tempted to reach for food because of emotions, please remind me that it will not satisfy me. I do thank You for food, but I turn to You for the spiritual food that truly satisfies. In Jesus' name, amen.

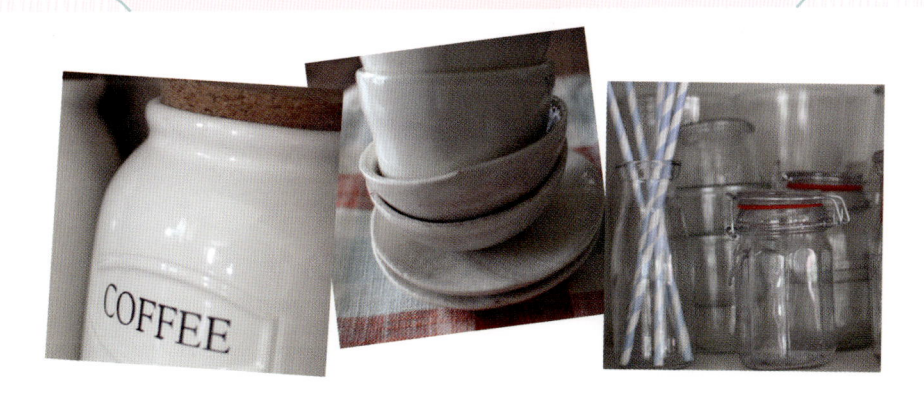

Dash of Inspiration

As far as your physical body is concerned, be sure you are getting plenty of protein and a good amount of fiber with each meal. These will better satisfy your hunger. There are times, though, when it is not truly physical hunger at all. In those times prayer, praise, and speaking the Word can be powerful tools to fill you emotionally and spiritually. I personally love to go on walks and spend time with the Lord, asking Him to strengthen me. The great thing about this is that He promises always to draw near to us when we draw near to Him. It is then that you have the true revelation that you truly can do *all* things through Christ who gives you strength!

17

Abide in God's Love

"Abide in Me, and I in you. As the branch cannot bear fruit by itself, unless it abides in the vine, neither can you, unless you abide in Me."
—JOHN 15:4 NKJV

Jesus explained in John 15:4 to His disciples—and to us today—that in order to bear fruit, we need to abide in Him. He paints a portrait of the relationship between a vine and a branch and points out that a branch by itself cannot produce fruit unless it is receiving nourishment from the vine. Similarly, we who name Jesus as our Savior and Lord cannot bear fruit unless we are receiving nourishment from Him.

So how do we abide in Jesus? The Bible says, "If anyone acknowledges that Jesus is the Son of God, God lives in them and they in God. And so we know and rely on the love God has for us. God is love. Whoever lives in love lives in God, and God in them" (1 John 4:15–16). We see here that the key to abiding in God and having God live in us is first asking Jesus to be our Lord and Savior. Then we choose to put our trust in God's love. If we abide in God's love, then we are abiding in Him.

One practical way to abide in the Lord is to spend time with Him each day. This can be done through prayer, reading the Word, and even praising God. When we do this, we are keeping our hearts connected to His!

This abiding also happens as we walk through life, seeking to love and serve others as Jesus loves us. As we choose to see the world and others through the lens of His love, our lives will impact others. And that is ultimately what being connected to the vine and bearing fruit is all about!

> **Lord, teach me** to grow and strengthen my relationship with You. Teach me to abide in You and Your love. As I do so, please pour Your love through me, that it may overflow onto those around me. I pray that my life will bear fruit for You that will last. In Jesus' name, amen.

18

People Pleasing

Am I now trying to win the approval of human beings, or of God? Or am I trying to please people? If I were still trying to please people, I would not be a servant of Christ.

—GALATIANS 1:10

A life of balance will not only glorify God, but it will also make us easier to live with at home! Often, though, we get out of balance and feel overwhelmed and stressed because we've said one simple word too often: *yes*.

Among the different reasons we find ourselves overcommitting is a fear of disappointing people, wanting to be well liked, or even a desire to please the Lord. The reality, however, is that we will let some people down, and other people will dislike us no matter what we do or don't do! Furthermore, God loves us unconditionally, and although our actions can be disappointing to Him, He will never stop loving us.

In light of these truths, let's try this before we say yes to anything: pause, give it some thought, consider our motives and how much stress it will add to our lives, ask God to guide us in our decision, and even ask for some time to think more about the opportunity. Only when our lives are in balance can we give our best to

God and our families. When our priorities line up with the Lord's priorities for us and we give our all to the things that matter most, we honor and bless the Lord. Let's learn to live for our all-important Audience of One.

Lord, I pray that You will give me the wisdom and the strength to say no when I need to. When an opportunity presents itself, please remind me of those things that are the most important in my life. Help me be a good steward of the time and talents You have entrusted to me. In Jesus' name, amen.

19

Let the Word Have Final Say

Pay attention to what I say;
    turn your ear to my words.
Do not let them out of your sight,
    keep them within your heart;
for they are life to those who find them
    and health to one's whole body.
Above all else, guard your heart,
    for everything you do flows from it.

—PROVERBS 4:20-23

We are bombarded by messages every day. Everything from movies and TV to magazines, advertisements, and the people around us shout opinions about who we should be and what our lives should look like. Even a few minutes on Facebook or other social media can fill your mind with images, stories, and snippets of information about what makes a person's life acceptable and meaningful. We need to recognize that the only true and accurate voice to listen to is the Word of God. Far superior to any wavering opinion of our culture, the Word of God offers an unchanging message as well as life-giving power.

If you are a Christian, the Spirit of Jesus lives inside of you. Although we are still living in this world, when we received Christ as our Savior, we became citizens of heaven and are, in a sense, no longer subject to the world's system. Yes, we still are to submit to authorities, pay taxes, and so forth (Romans 13:6). But what the world says about right and wrong, about values and morals, about styles and behaviors no longer pertains to you. The Word of God trumps the world's messages.

When you confront opinions and ideas that don't line up with the Word of God, remind yourself that Scripture is the ultimate authority for those who follow Jesus. One practical way to do this is to spend time with God each day. As you search through His Word, ask Him to show you promises about your situation. And as He reveals scriptures that apply to whatever it is that you are facing, write them down and post them where you can see them. Whenever you are tempted to feel discouraged or doubt what He spoke to you, go back and read those scriptures, knowing that no matter what message comes your way, the Word of God will always have the final say in your life.

Lord, I thank You that Scripture contains truth for life. Help me keep Your Word before my eyes and in my heart. I choose to trust in Your Word and build my life on its teachings. May its truth help me guard my heart against the lies around me that too many accept as truth. In Jesus' name, amen.

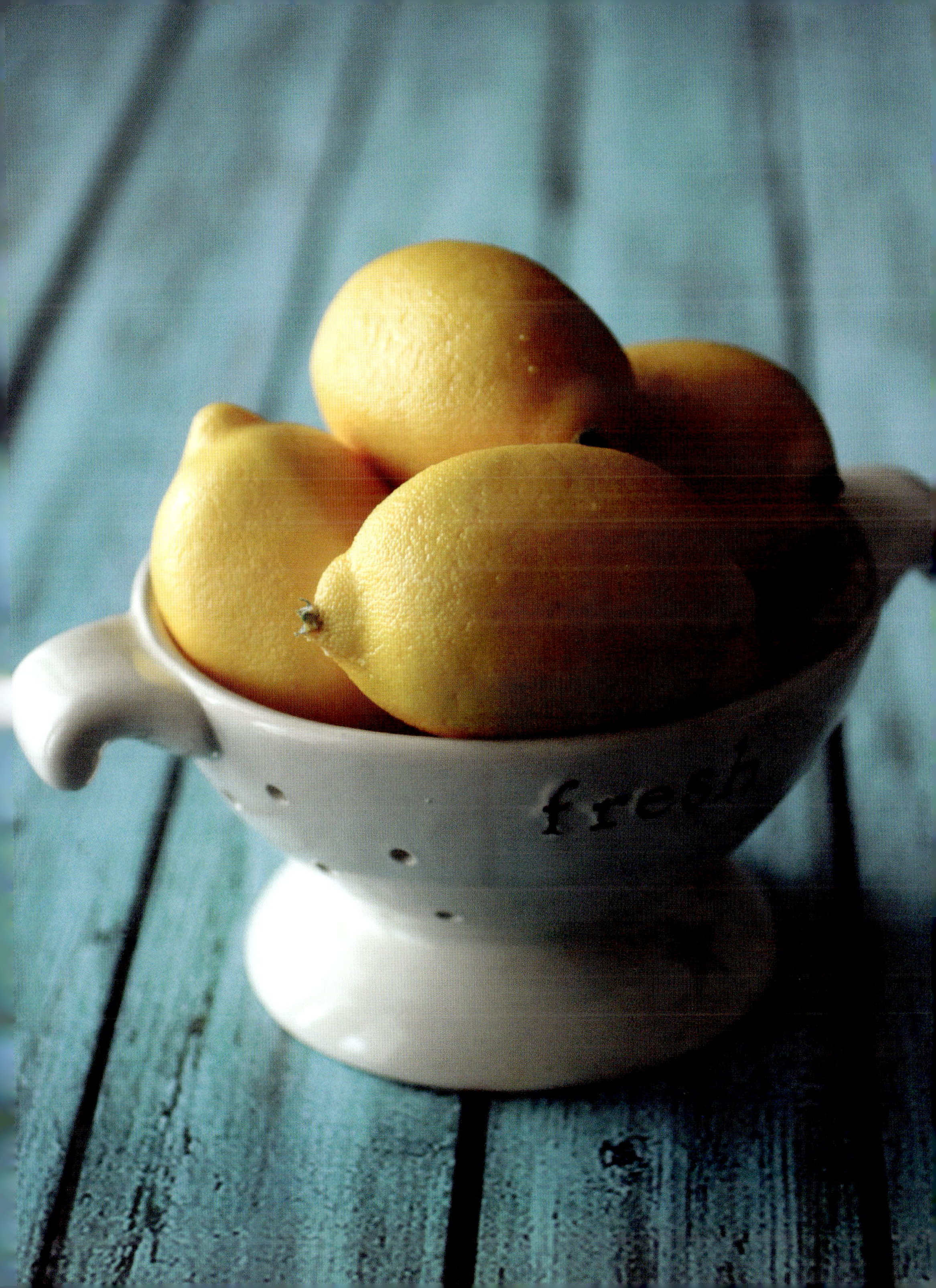
fresh

20

God Cares for You

Praise be to the God and Father of our Lord Jesus Christ, the Father of compassion and the God of all comfort, who comforts us in all our troubles, so that we can comfort those in any trouble with the comfort we ourselves receive from God.

—2 CORINTHIANS 1:3-4

God loves us so much. In fact, He *is* love. We may not always feel His love, but much of that has to do with our own hearts. Often our hearts have become hardened by the busyness of life, or we can become overwhelmed by the difficult times we're facing, and we don't seem to feel the warmth of God's embrace. In times like these, it is so important that we focus on promises like 2 Corinthians 1:3–4. God reminds us in this passage that He is the Source of all comfort. The best thing we can do, then, is spend time with Him every day, no matter how busy we are or how much we may be hurting. God will meet us where we are each day as we take time to meet with Him. He will comfort us whether we are stressed out, feeling burdened, or are going through a rough time.

The best part about God's comfort is that He is able to heal any wound, no matter how big or small, no matter its cause. And God's care for us doesn't stop there! This passage of Scripture explains that when we stay connected to our heavenly Father and He comforts us with His great love, we can then share His comfort and love with those we know who are hurting. What a beautiful design! God pours His compassion and comfort out *to* those of us who need it most and then pours that compassion and comfort *through* us to others who are hurting. Let's make the choice to stay connected daily to the God of compassion so we can share His love and compassion in this broken world.

> **Lord, I thank You** for working in my life to bring wholeness to my brokenness. Thank You for coming alongside me with Your comfort and compassion. Lord, I pray that when I receive Your love, You will then use me to go out and share that same love with others who need it. In Jesus' name, amen.

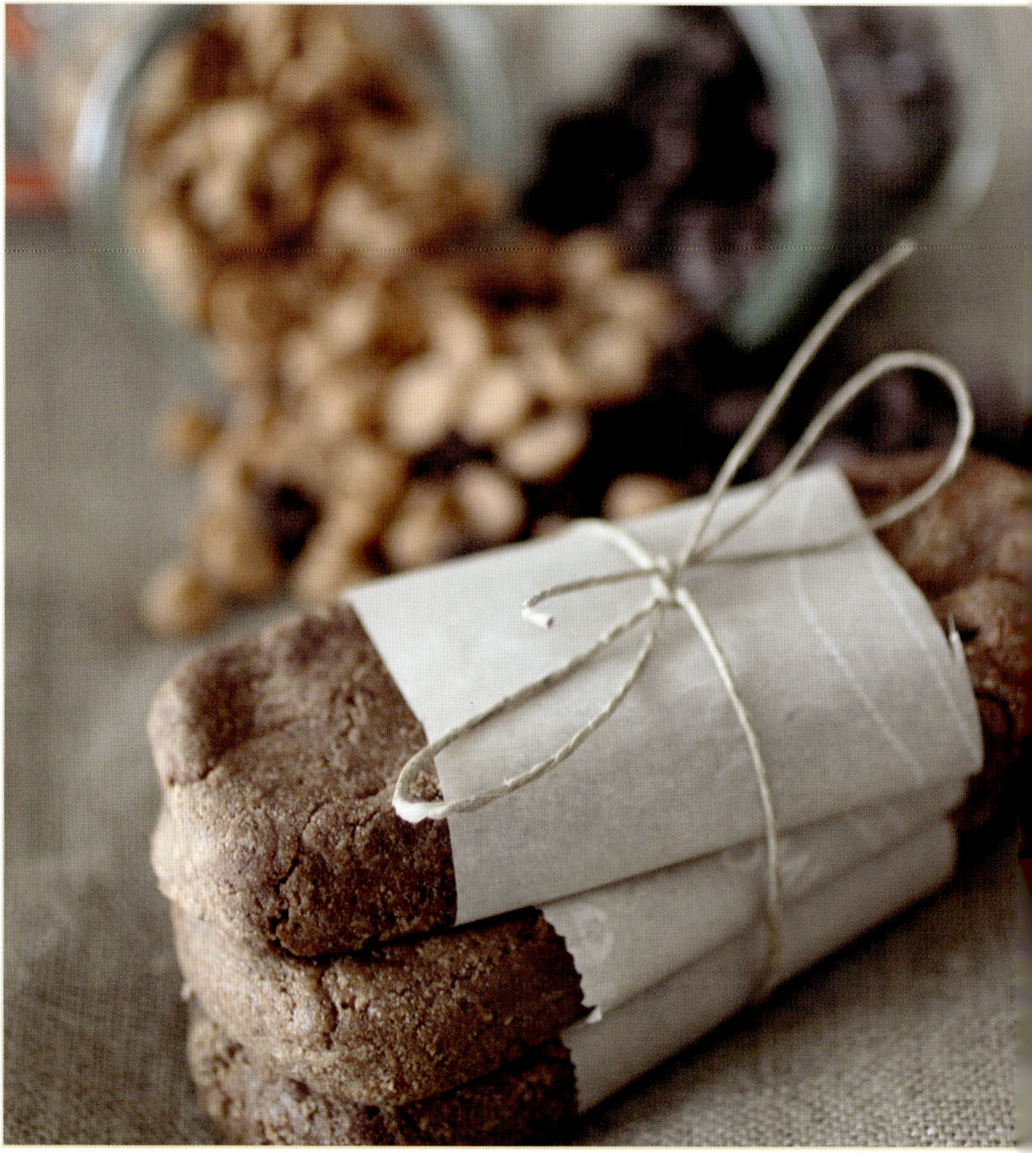

Chocolate Peanut Butter Protein Bar for One

INGREDIENTS:
2 tbs no-sugar-added maple syrup
¼ cup protein powder
1½ tbs peanut or almond flour
½ tbs unsweetened cocoa powder
pinch of salt

METHOD:
1. Spray a small bowl with nonstick cooking spray and pour syrup in bowl. Microwave syrup in the bowl for 30 seconds. Remove and quickly stir in the protein powder, flour, cocoa powder, and salt.
2. Work quickly to form mixture into a bar, and set on a piece of parchment paper or foil lightly sprayed with nonstick cooking spray so it won't stick. (Note: The reason you need to work fairly quickly is because it will get more sticky as it cools.) Let it come completely to room temperature, about 5 to 10 minutes, and enjoy immediately. Or wrap it in foil, or place in a ziplock bag, and enjoy as a delicious snack any time of day!

SERVINGS: 1 (1 bar per serving)

Finding Contentment

I am not saying this because I am in need, for I have learned to be content whatever the circumstances. I know what it is to be in need, and I know what it is to have plenty. I have learned the secret of being content in any and every situation, whether well fed or hungry, whether living in plenty or in want. I can do all this through him who gives me strength.
—PHILIPPIANS 4:11-13

At some point, it seems that we all find ourselves in a season when we are dissatisfied with where we are in life. Whether it is unhappiness with our jobs, our bodies, our marital status, or life in general, we find our attitudes shifting into a downward spiral. We think if we only had more or if circumstances were different, then we would finally be happy. This is a false sense of reality. If we don't learn to be content with what we have now, we will always find ourselves back in the place of discontentment and wanting more. It is critical to learn to be content with what we have and where we are.

As we see in Philippians, Paul was able to be content through Christ who gave him strength. Paul didn't naturally feel happy when he was hungry, but through Christ, he was able to change his perspective and choose thankfulness. In

Galatians 5:22–23, we see that we don't need to muster up happiness, but that God has planted joy inside of us: "The fruit of the Spirit is love, joy, peace, patience, kindness, goodness, faithfulness, gentleness, self-control" (NASB). Our flesh cries out for more of the things of the world and pouts with discontentment, but the more we discipline our flesh by not giving it worldly things, the better our attitude will be. We can fix our eyes on Jesus and claim the joy that the Holy Spirit blesses us with. When we make those choices, our attitude will be one of gratitude and praise.

What are some things that you thought might bring you contentment, but proved to be empty? Make a list of ways you could rethink your pursuit of contentment. Ask God to help you think and pray differently.

Lord, I ask You to forgive me for my discontentment in my present situation. I want to be aware of my blessings; I want to live with thankfulness. Help me realize how very blessed I am, for You have given me much. May I choose gratitude and contentment, I pray. In Jesus' name, amen.

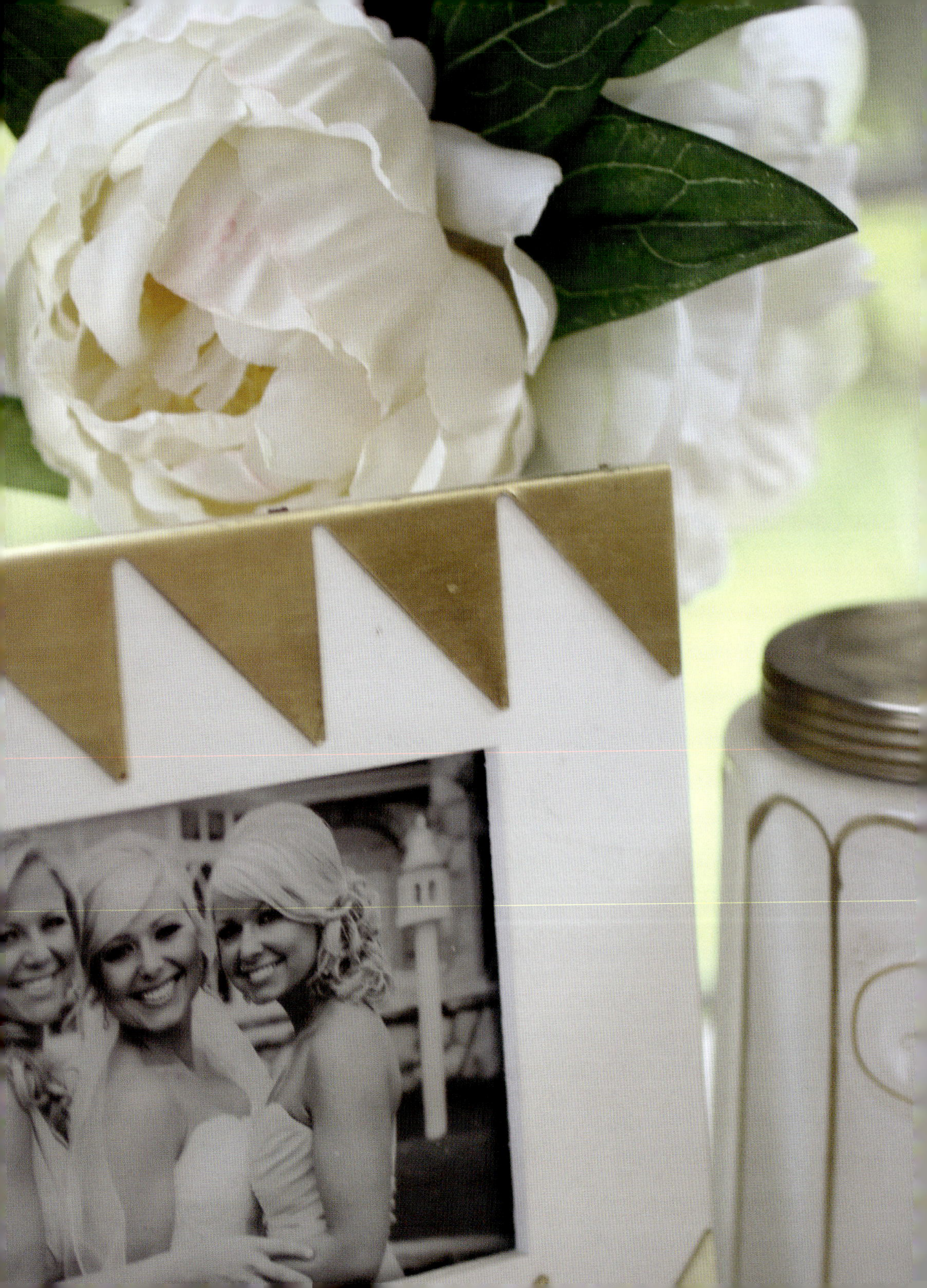

22

Submit Everything to God

Submit to God, and you will have peace;
then things will go well for you.
—JOB 22:21 NLT

The word *submission* is often misunderstood in our society. The misuse of submission in leadership has caused people to rebel against the idea of submitting to someone. Submission requires faith and trust in the person who is in leadership. But many people have a difficult time trusting others due to past hurts, so they don't ever humble themselves and admit they need help from a higher power. I used to think I could do it all on my own, which was a sense of pride, but it only left me continuously falling short and burdened with feelings of failure. I've learned that submission to God is simply a realization that I need Him in my life, and I don't ever have to fear trusting in Him.

If we submit every area of our life to God, then we don't need to try to figure things out on our own. We have the Lord's guarantee that if we surrender to Him, "things will go well" with us. We will have peace knowing that the plans He has for us (even in the area of our weight and health) are far greater than what we could ever accomplish on our own. God says in His Word, "'My thoughts are not your thoughts, neither are your ways my ways,' declares the Lord. 'As the heavens are higher than the earth, so are my ways higher than your ways and my thoughts than your thoughts'" (Isaiah 55:8–9). God has a better plan for our lives than we could ever imagine or map out ourselves. We honor God when, as an act of faith, we submit our lives and our very selves to Him.

> **Lord, help me surrender** every area of my life over to You so that I will find true peace. Specifically, I release _____ to Your control right now, knowing that I can trust it—and everything— to Your good and perfect care. In Jesus' name, amen!

23

Dealing with Temptation

God is faithful; he will not let you be tempted beyond what you can bear. But when you are tempted, he will also provide a way out so that you can stand up and endure it.

—1 CORINTHIANS 10:13

We are faced with temptations on a daily basis. Whether it be a temptation to gossip, to overeat, to lie, or to be lazy, the fleshly part of us is constantly crying out to get its own way, similar to a spoiled toddler. We are faced with a choice of giving in to our flesh or obeying God.

Although being tempted is a reality of life on this earth, this verse tells us that we can be the overcomers God has called us to be even in the midst of temptations and trials. In order to find our way out of a tempting situation, we need to determine what is happening when we find ourselves giving in to temptation, and the first step is being able to recognize Satan's schemes. Satan works overtime to draw us away from the fruits of the Spirit, some of which are peace, joy, love, gentleness, and self-control. He wants us to live with fear, doubt, stress, and anxiety, with our eyes focused on earthly circumstances rather than on the Lord. When the Holy Spirit isn't leading us, we are by default following our fleshly nature, which makes us more susceptible to temptation and sin.

The good news is that with the Holy Spirit as our Counselor, we don't have to be subject to our flesh! We can be overcomers by asking the Holy Spirit to help us see when we are stepping away from God and to then choose to walk with Him instead. When we find that we are drifting toward worry, doubt, fear, and stress, we need to make the choice to steer our hearts and minds back to God's peace, joy, and love. And we must continuously choose to rein in our emotions and cast our cares upon the Lord.

> **Lord, when I'm tempted** by Satan's schemes, please help me choose to rein in my emotions and cast my cares upon You. I thank You, Holy Spirit, for Your presence. And I thank You, Lord, for transforming me one day at a time. In Jesus' name, amen!

24

Get God Involved

Whether you eat or drink or whatever you do, do it all for the glory of God.
—1 CORINTHIANS 10:31

God truly does care about every area of our lives! In fact, as the Westminster Shorter Catechism stated way back in 1647, humans were created "to glorify God and to enjoy Him forever." The fact that we can actually give glory to God in our eating and drinking and in all of our actions shows that He wants us to be aware of Him in all things, even those we might consider mundane.

So how do we give God glory as we do our seemingly endless household chores? By thanking Him for the food we wash off plates, for plates to put food on, for people to share food with. By thanking Him for indoor plumbing and choosing not to grumble when we have to clean the bathroom—*again? already?*—and thanking Him for the people you love who make it dirty.

And what does giving God glory as we eat and drink look like? It's not simply about controlling our own eating because self-control is ultimately relying on self, not on God. We honor God when we let Him be Lord over every aspect of our lives—even what and how much we eat. Again, the issue is not about self-control, but Spirit-control—asking the Holy Spirit to help us with our food choices, to speak to us about when we have had enough, and to give us the strength to say no to foods that will not bring health to our bodies. When we listen to the Spirit of God regarding what we eat and drink, we are giving Him access and complete control over these areas of our lives. And that gives God glory!

> **Lord, I desire to glorify You** in every area of my life. I ask You to guide me so that every day, every meal, I will make wise choices regarding what I put in my body. Please help me know when I've had enough to eat and give me the strength to resist foods that are not healthy for the body You have entrusted to my care. In Jesus' name, amen!

Dash of Inspiration

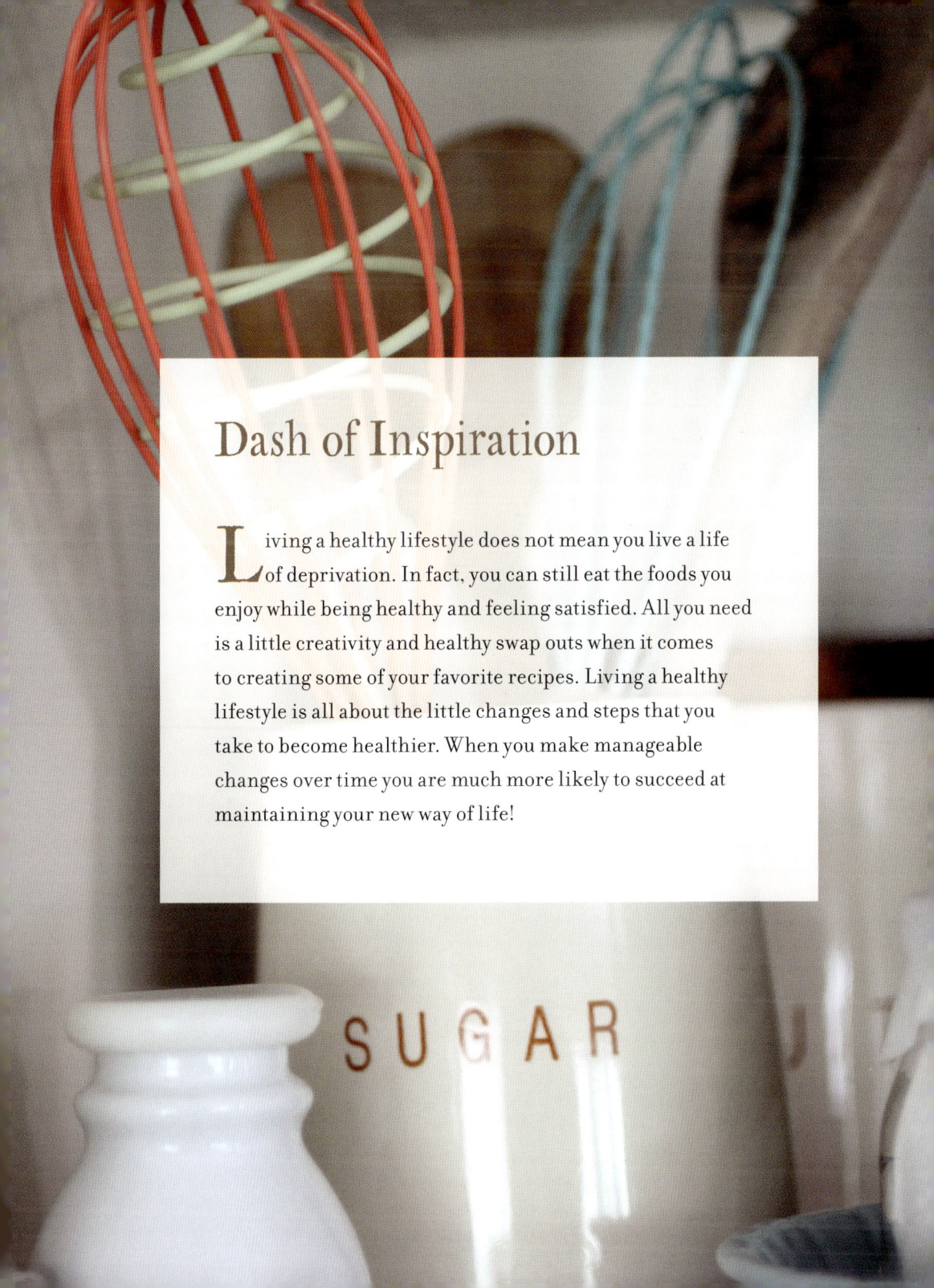

Living a healthy lifestyle does not mean you live a life of deprivation. In fact, you can still eat the foods you enjoy while being healthy and feeling satisfied. All you need is a little creativity and healthy swap outs when it comes to creating some of your favorite recipes. Living a healthy lifestyle is all about the little changes and steps that you take to become healthier. When you make manageable changes over time you are much more likely to succeed at maintaining your new way of life!

25

Speaking Words of Life

The tongue can bring death or life;
those who love to talk will reap the consequences.
—PROVERBS 18:21 NLT

God created the heavens, the earth, and everything in them with His words (Hebrews 11:3). Isn't that amazing—that the sun, moon, and stars could be spoken into existence? And since we were created in the image of God, our words, when spoken in faith, have the power to create as well. There is no such thing as words without meaning. Each word we speak will produce either life or death.

When we speak the Word of God in faith, it can be one of our most powerful weapons against the devil (Ephesians 6:17). The Bible also says that faith-filled words can move mountains (Mark 11:23). And in Matthew 8, we see Jesus marvel at the Roman centurion's uncommon faith in the authority of Jesus' spoken Word—that the centurion's servant would be healed simply by Jesus speaking.

If we speak with words that line up with God's Word, we will begin to see the positive results that follow. But if we continue to speak words of doubt, we will eventually believe them and experience the negative consequences these words produce. Death and life truly are in the power of every word we speak. As we go about our day today, let us choose to use encouraging words that will build up those those around us. How will you use your words today?

> **Lord, please help me** use my words to create life. Please show me, Holy Spirit, when I am speaking words of doubt, fear, or destruction, and help me guard my mouth. I thank You that when I speak Your Word, it will produce life in me and in the world around me. In Jesus' name, amen!

Sparkling Strawberry Slushie

INGREDIENTS:
2 cups frozen strawberries (or other frozen fruit)
1 cup lemon or lime sparkling water
2 to 3 packets stevia (or sweetener to taste)
Optional: freshly squeezed lemon juice to taste

METHOD:
1. Place all ingredients in the blender and blend until smooth.
2. Pour into 2 glasses and enjoy with a straw or spoon!

SERVINGS: 2 (1 slushie per serving)

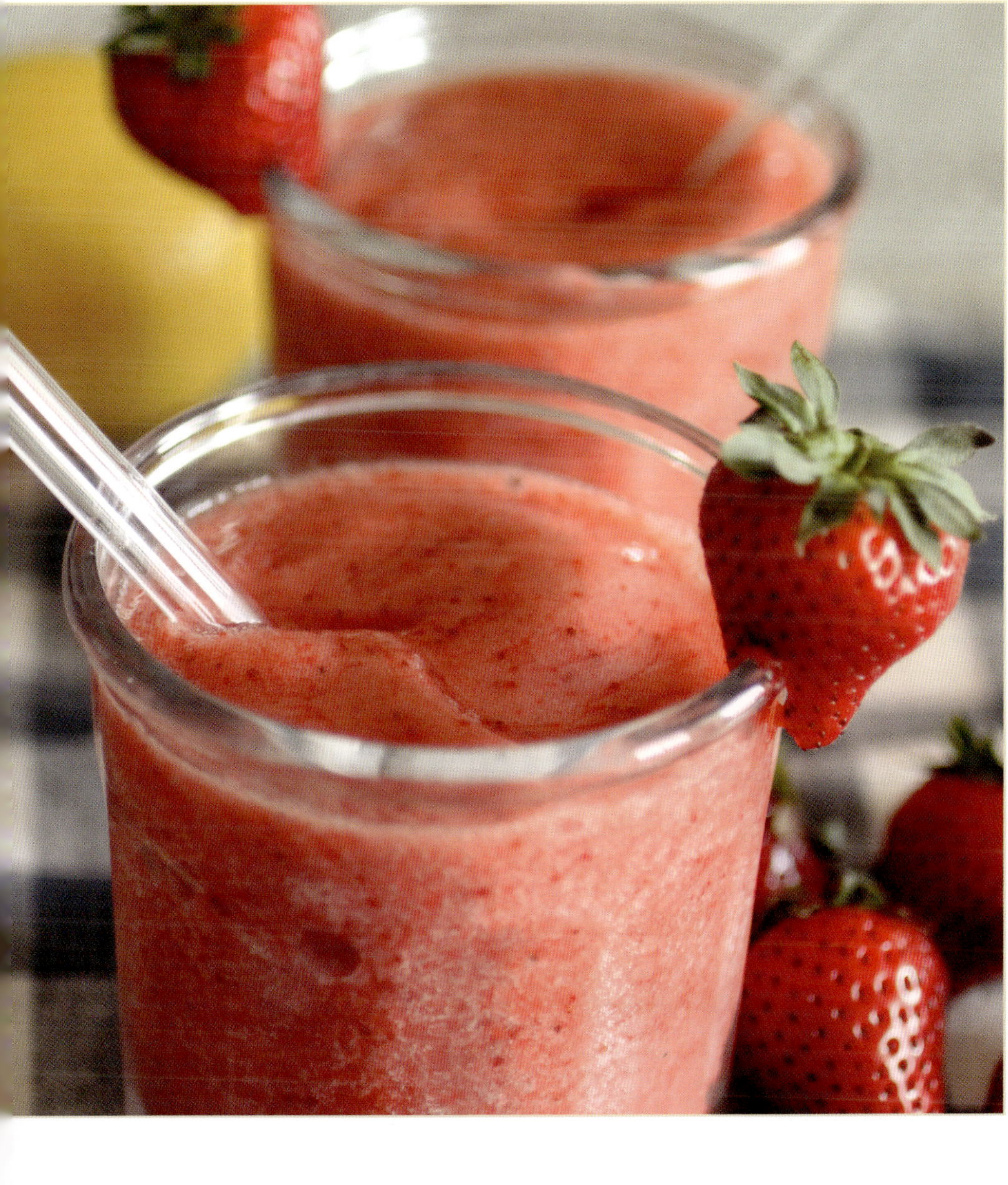

26

Depend on God's Strength

That's why I work and struggle so hard, depending on Christ's mighty power that works within me.
—**COLOSSIANS 1:29** NLT

Do you have a hard time trusting God? With the little things? The big things? Why is it so difficult? For me, one of the hardest things to trust God with was my weight. For years I tried to control my weight by doing everything I knew to do in my own strength and wisdom, which always led to feelings of burnout and failure. Although it was a difficult lesson to learn, I realized that I had to turn this area of my life over to the Lord, and it was then that I found true strength and victory.

In everything we do, we should trust in, lean on, and depend on Christ's mighty power that is at work within us. When we serve and obey God, He has promised to bless whatever we set our hands to (Deuteronomy 28:1, 8). But in order for Him to bless our work, we must take action and put our hands to doing his will. From there, we can rest assured that He is giving us His power to accomplish the task.

God's Word also promises that we can do all things through Him who gives us strength (Philippians 4:13). This promise combined with Deuteronomy 28:8 teaches that we don't need to beg God to help us accomplish a goal we are working toward. Rather, we have His promise that if we do our part (work at something that follows His will), then He will do His part (provide us with the strength and power to reach that goal). When we depend on God and His power, we can be sure that we'll overcome any trial or hardship that comes our way.

> **Lord, please help me see** that You are working in and through me so that I don't depend on my own wisdom, strength, or ability. Remind me to trust in Your mighty power that is at work in me to accomplish all that I set my hand to. In Jesus' name, amen!

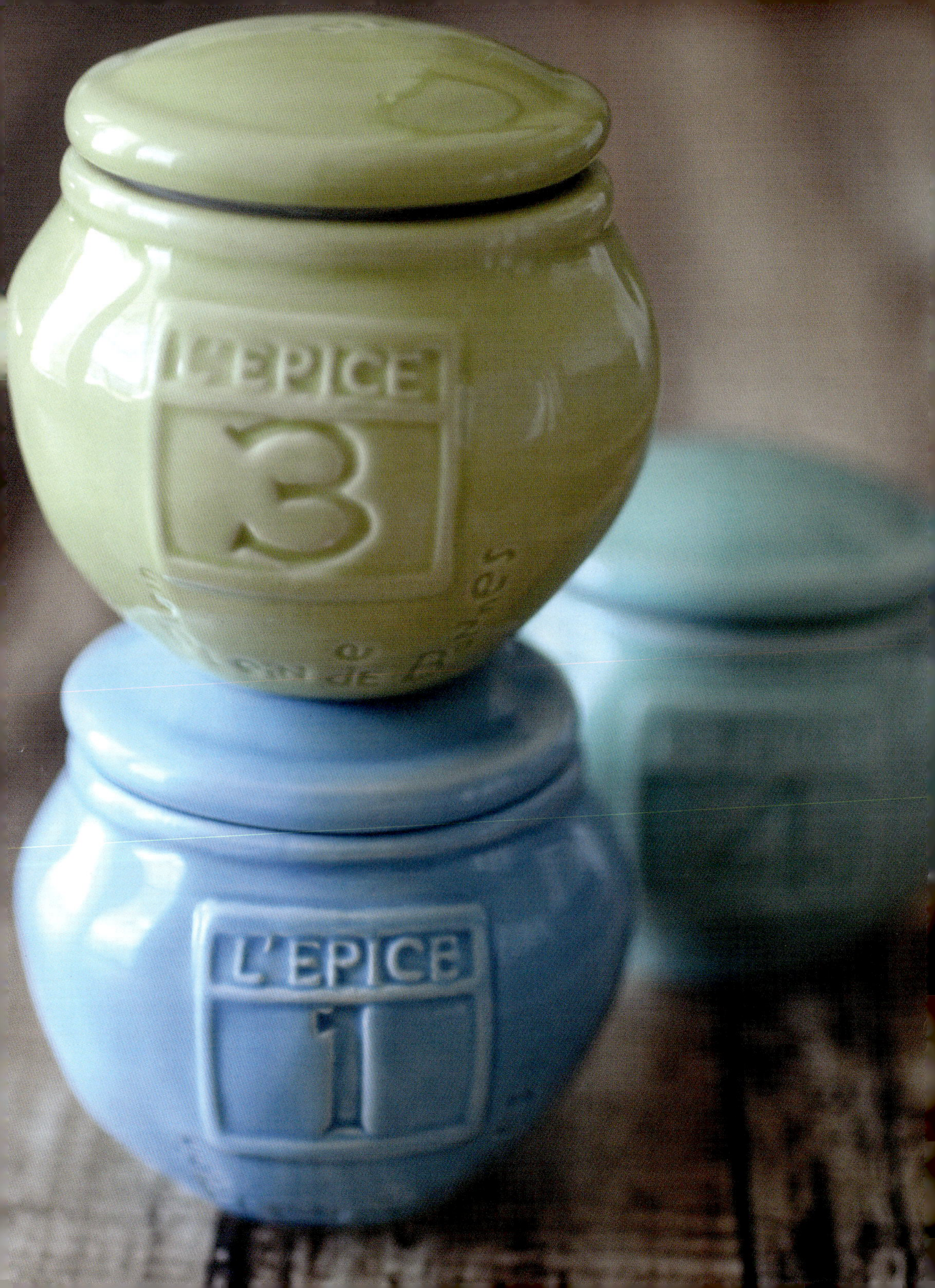
L'EPICE
3
L'EPICE
1

27

Empowered by God

"Not by might nor by power, but by my Spirit," says the Lord Almighty.
—ZECHARIAH 4:6

I have found that when life starts to get really busy, hectic, and out of control, I tend to try to muster up enough power and might to get through it on my own. Can you relate?

Even if we *could* make it through the tough times in our own strength, why would we want to? Zechariah 4:6 clearly points us to the most reliable Source of power: the Spirit of God! The great news is this: "The Spirit of God, who raised Jesus from the dead, lives in you" (Romans 8:11 NLT). If we simply acknowledge and believe and turn to Him in faith, God will act in our lives. It is then that we can be empowered by Him!

Lord, thank You for sending Your Spirit to live inside of me— to comfort me, guide me, teach me, and empower me! Help me recognize that Your Spirit is a mighty power source and is all I need to get through any situation in life. In Jesus' name, amen.

28

Weathering the Storms of Life

[Jesus] said to his disciples, "Why are you so afraid? Do you still have no faith?"
—MARK 4:40

Peace is so hard to come by in today's world. When we are surrounded by world events that stir our fears and hear news stories of destruction and terror, it is hard to have peace of mind. It becomes even more difficult when those storms hit close to home. When we face financial stress or lose a loved one, peace seems even more out of reach. However, as difficult as it may be, God calls us to live in peace. He wants us to be at peace, even in the midst of difficult times. The great news is that we can have peace at all times because He promises to help us.

To be at peace, we must remain confident in God and in His ability to calm the storms in our lives. In Mark 4, the disciples were in a boat with Jesus when a terrible storm hit. As the disciples looked at the increasing wind and growing waves, they panicked. Jesus was sleeping—right through the violent storm! The frightened disciples woke Jesus and begged Him to save them. Jesus calmed the storm and then rebuked the disciples, asking why they had been so afraid. After all, the One who controls the wind and the waves was there in the boat with them!

Likewise, when we start to look at the wind and the waves in our own lives, we can too easily take our eyes off the One who gave us life. We lose sight of how great our God is and of His mighty power to work on our behalf. But we have an option: instead of being filled with fear, worry, or doubt during the storms of life, we can turn to Jesus, trusting that He is in the boat of life with us and that He will show us what we need to do to survive the storm. We can also trust Jesus to calm the storm inside our hearts and enable us to listen for His guidance and direction—and then do what He says.

> **Lord, I praise You** for Your ability to calm the storms in my life. I know that You are more than able to guide me safely through each situation, but sometimes I forget. Help me remember that You are right here with me. I want to place my faith only in You. In Jesus' name, amen.

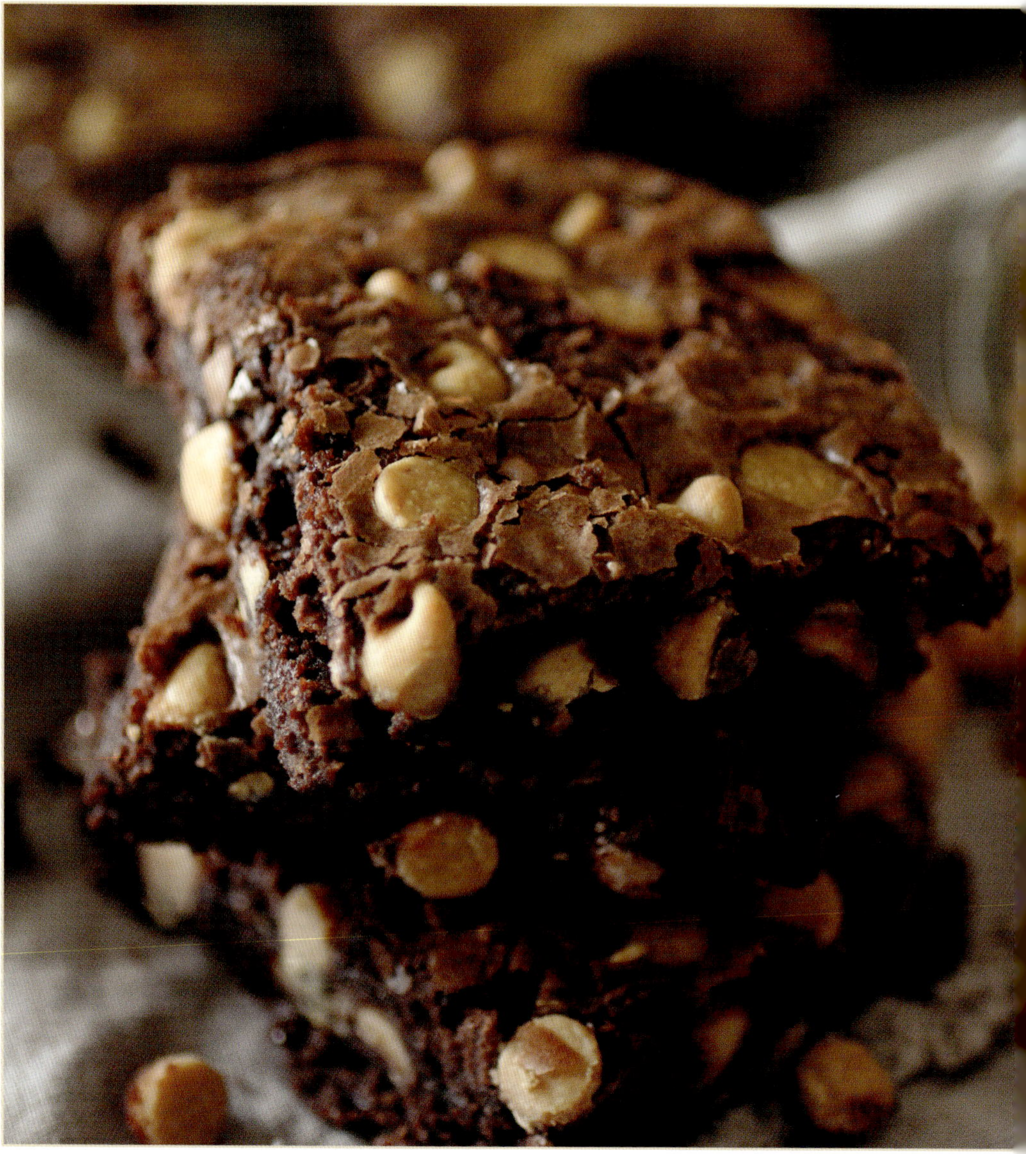

Flourless Peanut Butter Chip Brownies

INGREDIENTS:
1 (15-ounce) can black beans, drained and rinsed well (other beans will also work)
2 large eggs
2 tbs peanut butter, melted
¼ cup low-sugar maple syrup or honey
1 tsp white vinegar
½ cup unsweetened cocoa powder
¾ cup baking stevia (or 1½ cups sweetener that measures like sugar)
½ tsp baking powder
½ tsp baking soda
¼ tsp salt
¼ cup peanut butter chips

METHOD:
1. Preheat oven to 350 degrees. Spray a 9 x 9-inch baking pan with nonstick cooking spray. Place beans, eggs, peanut butter, syrup, vinegar, cocoa powder, stevia, baking powder, baking soda, and salt into a blender or food processor and blend batter until it is completely smooth. Stir in peanut butter chips and pour mixture into the baking pan, spreading it out evenly.
2. Bake for 18 to 22 minutes, or until a toothpick comes out clean (a few crumbs are okay, but it shouldn't be wet). Let cool completely, and cut into 9 brownies. Store leftovers in the fridge for up to 7 days, or in the freezer for up to 1 month.

SERVINGS: 9 (1 brownie per serving)

29

Forgetting What Is Behind

Not that I have already obtained all this, or have already arrived at my goal, but I press on to take hold of that for which Christ Jesus took hold of me. Brothers and sisters, I do not consider myself yet to have taken hold of it. But one thing I do: Forgetting what is behind and straining toward what is ahead, I press on toward the goal to win the prize for which God has called me heavenward in Christ Jesus.

—PHILIPPIANS 3:12-14

All of us have moments in our past that we would love to forget: people who let us down, past mistakes and failures, and more. I know I'm not the only one who has wished I could press the do-over button at some point! Recalling past memories of defeat can lead to present feelings of failure.

Problems arise when we meditate on those low moments. There was a time in my life when I kept looking at my past with feelings of guilt that I ever let myself go down certain roads. When I slipped just a little bit in that same area, I couldn't help but feel completely defeated. Rather than looking at how far I've come, I would feel guilty about my past. Meditating on those low moments causes us to miss what God is doing *now* and, in our preoccupation, ignore the promises He has for our future. In Philippians 3:12–14, we see that although Paul hadn't arrived at the place he desired to be, he was determined to forget what was behind and to instead reach for what was ahead. We must stop looking behind us and start looking at what God has for us—today and in all the tomorrows to come.

Lord, please heal my heart and the wounds of my soul. Help me fix my eyes on what You are doing now. Remove anything that would keep me from moving according to the plan that You have for me. I thank You that I do not have to live tied to my past. In Jesus' name, amen.

30

Overcome Discouragement

Why, my soul, are you downcast?
> Why so disturbed within me?

Put your hope in God,
> for I will yet praise him,
> my Savior and my God.

—PSALM 42:5

Do you ever face discouragement? I've had days when out of the blue discouragement begins to bombard my thoughts, and feelings of defeat and failure flood my mind. It is then when I remember Psalm 42:5 and realize that the power is in where I put my focus. I have found that I simply can't stay discouraged when I praise God and focus on the awesome things He has done for me. Here in Psalm 42, the psalmist was also discouraged, but he reminded himself that his sadness would not last forever. Yes, he was "downcast," but he was confident that the Lord would turn his circumstances around and he would again have many reasons to praise his Savior and his God. Not only does praise take our attention off of our circumstances, but it also shifts our thoughts toward the strength and help we receive from the Lord when we place our trust in Him.

One simple and practical way to enter into praise is to play worship music and sing along! We can also praise without music by simply thanking God for His kindness and reflecting on the good things He has done for us. Even if it doesn't seem like we have much to praise God for, we can always thank Him for the amazing gift of His Son. It's because of Jesus' death on the cross that we can be called God's children and spend eternity with Him!

If you are facing a tough situation today, if you find yourself losing hope, if your emotions are sinking for no specific reason, take heart! In His gift of Jesus, God has provided all we need to be joyful and have peace no matter what circumstances we are facing!

Lord, please help me focus my attention on Your promises rather than on circumstances. Help me remember the truths of Your Word. I ask that You would help me overcome discouragement and be aware of all that I can praise You for today. In Jesus' name, amen.

You Have a Purpose

So, my dear brothers and sisters, be strong and immovable. Always work enthusiastically for the Lord, for you know that nothing you do for the Lord is ever useless.
—1 CORINTHIANS 15:58 NLT

As long as we are working for the Lord, then nothing we do—big or small—is ever wasted. In a society where success is measured by status, wealth, and appearance, this truth is crucial for us to remember. For those of us who live typical, everyday lives, it may be difficult to look at the challenges of a day and feel that we have accomplished something of note. When we find ourselves striving to do more, or when we feel we aren't doing anything that matters, we need to remind ourselves of this truth: we are serving the Lord. If we go about our daily tasks—chores around the house, preparing food for our families, changing diapers and wiping tears, making time for physical activity, or serving faithfully at our jobs—with a mind-set of serving the Lord with enthusiasm, then we are definitely doing something significant, and He is pleased. So the next time you pull out the mop, do it for the glory of the One who made you!

Lord, I dedicate to You the works of my hands and everyday tasks—big and small. Keep me mindful that I work for You and enthusiastic about that fact. I thank You, too, that in Your economy, nothing I do will be useless. In Jesus' name, amen.

Brownie Batter Overnight Protein Oatmeal

INGREDIENTS:

1 cup unsweetened almond milk (or low-fat milk of choice)

½ cup plain low-fat Greek yogurt (or mashed banana or applesauce)

2 tbs unsweetened cocoa powder

⅛ tsp salt

2 tbs baking stevia (or ¼ cup sweetener that measures like sugar)

1 cup old-fashioned oats

¼ cup protein powder (or additional oats)

topping of choice, optional

METHOD:

1. In a small bowl mix together the almond milk, yogurt, cocoa powder, salt, stevia, oats, and protein powder.
2. Divide between 2 small bowls, mugs, or mason jars. Cover and refrigerate overnight (or at least an hour or more) so the oats soften and absorb the liquid.
3. Top with chopped nuts or topping of choice, if desired. Enjoy cold, or microwave for 30 to 60 seconds to enjoy warm.

SERVINGS: 2

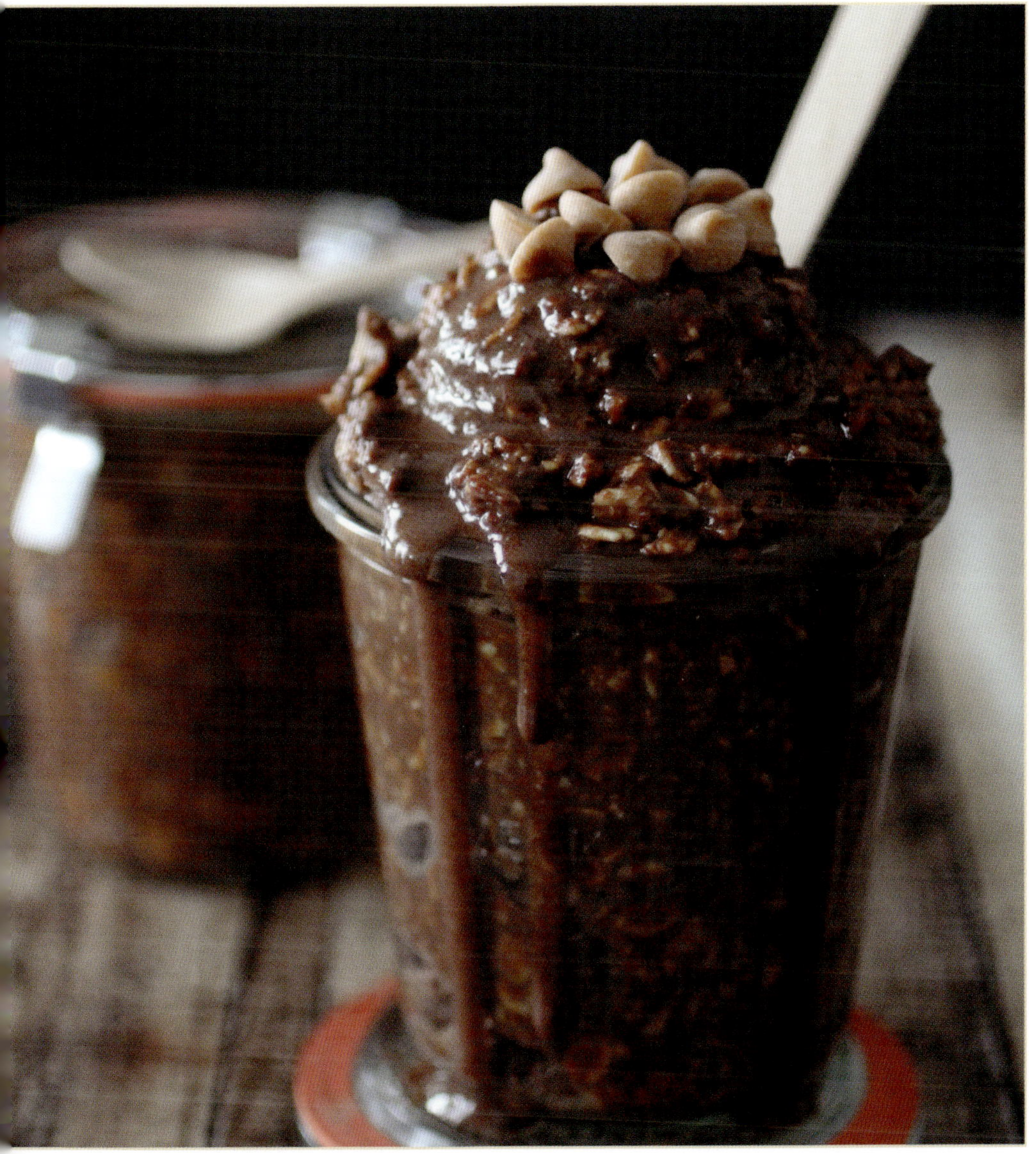

32

He Makes All Things New

Behold, I am doing a new thing;
>   now it springs forth, do you not perceive it?
I will make a way in the wilderness
>   and rivers in the desert.

—ISAIAH 43:19 ESV

If only we could push a magic button to restore relationships, heal heartache, repair the fallout from abandonment and emotional brokenness, and wipe away our failures. I have a feeling that button would get a lot of use! The good news is that we can find that kind of power in God's Word.

You see, the Word of God says that when we accept Christ as our Savior, we become a new creation. The old has passed away and the new has come (2 Corinthians 5:17 ESV). This means that the moment we surrender our lives to God, He takes away all of our past sins, failures, regrets, and hurts, and He gives us a new beginning. We now have a clean slate, and our sins have been forgiven.

What God accomplishes through one's salvation—this fresh start, this blessed newness—proves that He loves to rebuild, restore, and make all things new. At His core, God is all about restoration. If we look at the different seasons, for example, we can see a beautiful depiction of His handiwork. In the winter it may look as though everything is dead and withered, but when springtime arrives, we can see the new life budding, making all things new!

If we're honest, much of the time restoration doesn't seem possible. But the Lord promises in His Word that what is impossible with man is possible with God (Luke 18:27). Where we may see no hope in our current circumstances, we must choose to trust that God is working on our behalf, that He is our Defender and our Keeper, and that He never leaves us or forsakes us. Rather than focusing on circumstances, keep your eyes on our all-loving, all-powerful God. Trust that if He is able to turn winter into spring, then He is able to restore the broken places in your life as well.

> **Lord, I can't turn back** the hands of time or fix my current situation, but I know You can redeem and repair. I thank You that You are able to make all things new and to even make something beautiful out of my current situation. In Jesus' name, amen.

33

Renewing Your Mind

Do not conform to the pattern of this world, but be transformed by the renewing of your mind. Then you will be able to test and approve what God's will is—his good, pleasing and perfect will.

ROMANS 12:2

Have you believed a lie about yourself or about some aspect of your life? Perhaps the lie was about your appearance or how well you're doing as a wife or mother. Perhaps the lie was about whether your future is secure or even how God feels about you. Lies can come through another person's words or even our own thoughts. If we are experiencing anything less than what God promises in His Word—which is abundant life (John 10:10)—chances are, we are believing a lie or two. We must begin to recognize those lies and reject them.

The Bible says that Satan is the father of lies (John 8:44), and we must refuse to listen to his lies any longer! Once we recognize the lies we have believed, we can replace them with truth from God's Word. It is this knowledge of what God says is true—and what is true about us—that ultimately sets us free. God will do a good work in each of us, will renew our minds, and will change us from the inside out as we seek and pursue His will. Our enemy is real and comes to steal, kill, and destroy. Among his targets are our joy, peace, faith, hope, contentment, and confidence in God's love for us. But the good news is that Jesus came so we could have all those things!

Starting today, choose to believe what God says about your value to Him and His love for you. Believing the lies only furthers Satan's destructive work; choosing to believe the truth of God's Word enables us to know full and abundant life in Him. When we focus on the truth of Scripture, God uses it to refresh our spirit. And those truths become a rich soil where God's promises for us can flourish and the weeds of the enemy's lies cannot even take root.

> **Lord, please show me** the lies I have believed. I pray that You would reveal to me the truth in Your Word that can set me free from those lies. Use Scripture to transform me by renewing my mind, by replacing Satan's lies with Your life-giving truth. I want to know the abundant life You have created me to experience. In Jesus' name, amen!

Dash of Inspiration

It's amazing how our thoughts can shape our lives. I know how freeing it was for me to stop listening to lies and start thinking about God's truth. Every time you have a negative thought today, replace it with a truth. God loves you. You are fearfully and wonderfully made. God has good plans for you!

If you ever find yourself getting into negative thinking of any kind or are having a bad day, I encourage you to look up—God has good plans for you, but He needs you to trust Him and listen to His leading, which is hard to do with your head hanging down. And look out—the world is full of people who need the gifts and talents that you possess!

34

The Danger of Jealousy

But if you are bitterly jealous and there is selfish ambition in your heart, don't cover up the truth with boasting and lying. For jealousy and selfishness are not God's kind of wisdom. . . . For wherever there is jealousy and selfish ambition, there you will find disorder and evil of every kind.

—JAMES 3:14-16 NLT

Have you ever thought, *Wow! I wish I had that—or looked like that—or had that skill or talent*? Chances are that pretty much everyone has had thoughts like these at one time or another. But those thoughts are not a good path to walk down. And whether we realize it or not, comparing ourselves to others can make us feel insecure, jealous, and discontented.

James 3:14–16 teaches that when we operate in jealousy and selfishness, we are not operating in the wisdom of God. We also see in this verse that when we open the door to jealousy, we are opening the door for "disorder and evil of every kind" to operate in our lives. And once that door is opened, it can be difficult to close.

So how are we to deal with jealous thoughts and emotions? First, we must recognize them. We can ask the Lord to show us when we are having these thoughts. Once we recognize our jealousy, we must choose to take those thoughts captive and make them obedient to the truth of God's Word (2 Corinthians 10:5).

We must replace our jealous and envious thoughts that lead to destruction with thoughts of God's truth about what matters most and how much we matter to Him. A great way to replace these destructive, jealous thoughts is to think about who God created you to be. God designed you with a specific purpose in mind. He made you with every unique trait that you need to fulfill your special role on this earth. So the next time you find yourself feeling jealous, ask God to remind you that you are wonderfully made.

> **Lord, please stop me** when I begin to compare myself to others, when I start to walk that path to jealousy. Help me take those thoughts captive and focus instead on the truth of Your Word, which says that I am loved by the Creator of this world (1 John 4:19). What could matter more? In Jesus' name, amen.

35

The Fruit of Self-Control

The fruit of the Spirit is love, joy, peace, forbearance, kindness, goodness, faithfulness, gentleness and self-control.
—GALATIANS 5:22-23

If we have received Christ as our Savior, then the Holy Spirit—the Spirit of God—now lives inside of us (Acts 2:38). When the Holy Spirit comes to live in us, He comes bearing a gift—almost like a guest bringing a fruit basket. In order to enjoy the fruit, however, we must *choose* to yield to the Spirit of God inside us: "Walk by the Spirit, and you will not gratify the desires of the flesh" (Galatians 5:16). The fruits that will grow as we choose to follow the lead of God's Spirit are "love, joy, peace, forbearance, kindness, goodness, faithfulness, gentleness and self-control" (Galatians 5:22–23). That means that each one of us is able to have—among other qualities—self-control in any situation if we allow ourselves be led by the Spirit!

So how can we be led by the Spirit? We must first believe that He is inside us and that He is leading and guiding us into all truth (John 16:13). When we choose to both listen to the Spirit's still, small voice inside of us and then lean on His strength, we will be walking by the Spirit. It can take some time to learn to walk by the Spirit. Some practical ways to strengthen your spiritual muscles are to pray, read your Bible, worship, and fast. As we follow the Spirit of God, His fruit will flourish in our lives.

Are there any particular areas where you are struggling with self-control? If so, ask the Lord to help you draw out the fruit of self-control that is on the inside of you. Remember, it is a gift that has been freely given to you, but you need to make the choice to use it!

> **Lord, thank You** for Your willingness to guide my decisions, my steps, and my life! Enable me to choose throughout this day to follow You in every area of life. Thank You, Spirit of God, that as I walk with You, Your fruit will grow in me. Please use it to bless others. In Jesus' name, amen.

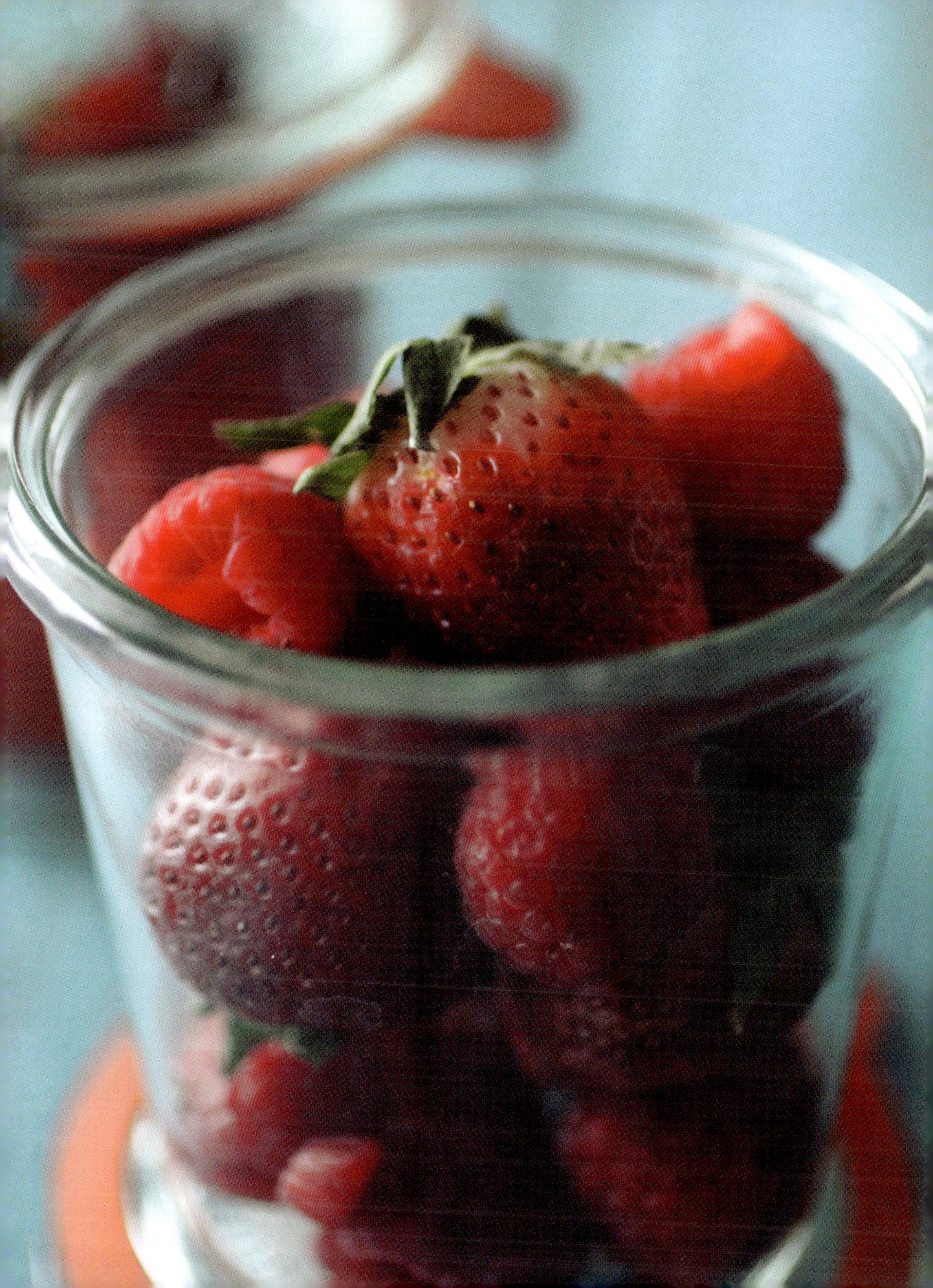

36

You Can Overcome

Little children, you are from God and have overcome [spirits who do not acknowledge Jesus], for he who is in you is greater than he who is in the world.
—1 JOHN 4:4 ESV

If we have received Jesus as our Savior, then we are children of God. And, according to 1 John 4:4, if we are God's children, then we are overcomers! When we ask Jesus to come into our hearts and be Lord of our lives, He comes to live inside of us. Think of it—the Creator of the universe has come to live inside of you and me!

So we must ask ourselves, is there anything that God can't overcome? Is there any trial that is too great for God to handle? The answer is a resounding no! So what does that mean for His children? It means that because He lives inside us, we are able to overcome the trials that we face with His help and guidance.

It's time that we start believing this scripture and take it as a personal truth. We must begin to see ourselves as victors and overcomers, because in Christ we are able to overcome everything in this world. We can do *all* things through Christ who lives in us. Praise God!

Lord, I thank You that I am an overcomer because You live inside of me. Help me see myself in You instead of viewing myself with my own limited ability. In Jesus' name, amen.

37

Honoring God

Don't be impressed with your own wisdom.
> Instead, fear the Lord and turn away from evil.

Then you will have healing for your body
> and strength for your bones.

—**PROVERBS 3:7-8** NLT

Many times the word *fear* refers to a negative emotion. However, when the Bible tells us to "fear the Lord," it means something completely different. In fact, this type of fear is not an emotion at all; rather, it is an action or attitude.

The fear of the Lord is the act of choosing to revere and honor Him. We first take this kind of action when we recognize that He alone is God. When we acknowledge that He—who is Lord of all—knows better than we do and that ultimately His ways are higher than ours, we can then submit freely to His leading. When we come to that place of humbleness, choosing to live God's way, we will receive the blessings of healing, restoration, and strength that can only come from Him.

Lord, forgive me for thinking I am wise and keep me from buying into the wisdom of this world. Instead, teach me to live in fear and reverence of You and in submission to Your leading. And thank You that You promise to bring healing and strength to me when I do so. In Jesus' name, amen.

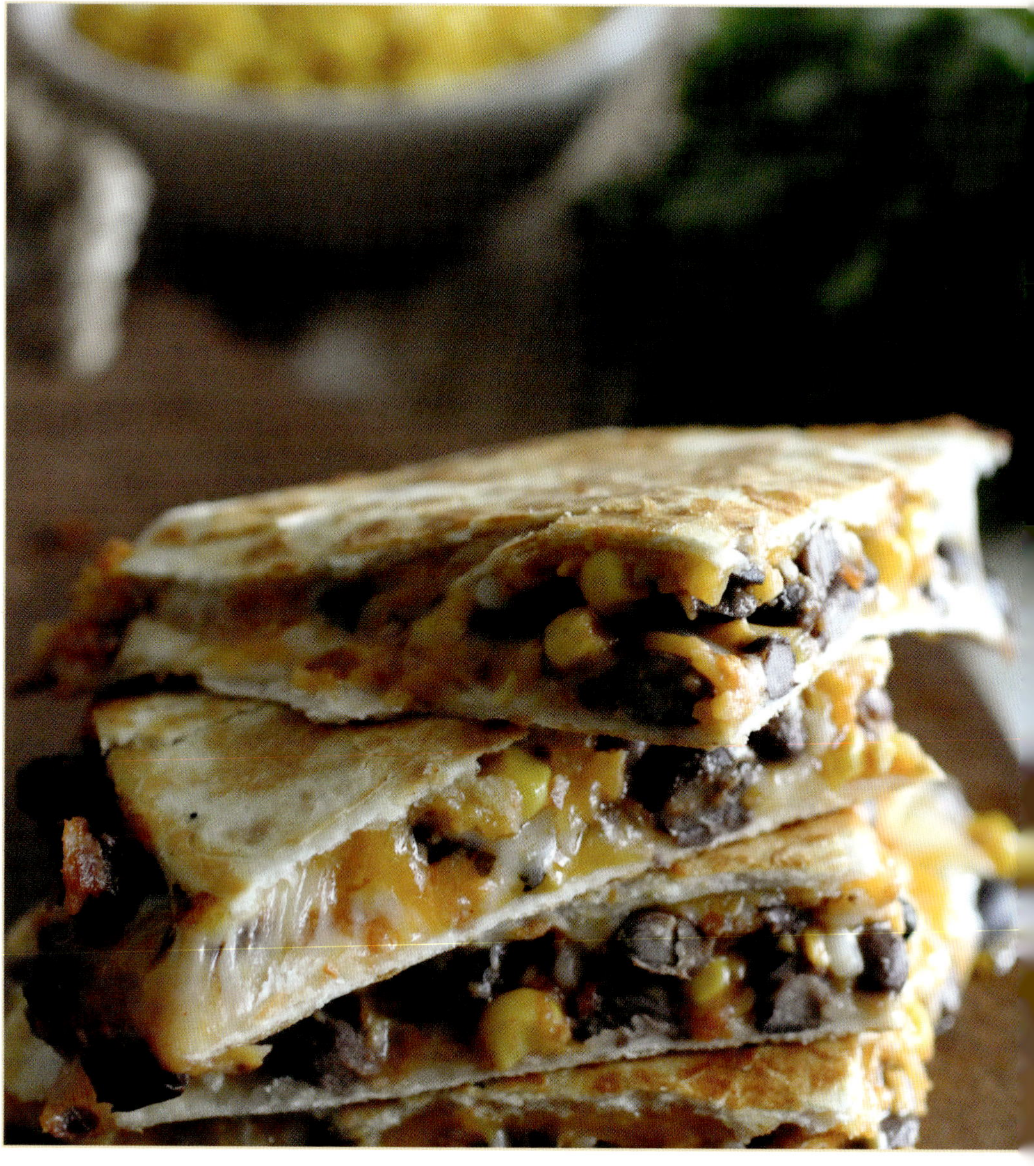

10-Minute Black Bean & Corn Quesadillas

INGREDIENTS:
1 (15-ounce) can black beans, rinsed and drained
1 cup corn
⅓ cup salsa
2 tsp taco seasoning
¼ cup fresh cilantro, chopped (or green onions)
1 cup shredded cheese of choice
8 whole grain tortillas

METHOD:
1. In a medium bowl mix together beans, corn, salsa, taco seasoning, and cilantro.
2. Preheat a large skillet over medium-low heat, and spray with nonstick cooking spray. Place one tortilla in the skillet, and scoop ½ cup of the filling onto the tortilla in the pan. Sprinkle ¼ cup cheese over the bean mixture, and place a second tortilla on top of the cheese. Press down on the top tortilla lightly with the back of your spatula so you can meld the tortillas together as the cheese melts. When the bottom tortilla begins to brown, flip the quesadilla over until both tortillas are lightly browned and crispy, and the cheesy filling has melted. Cut into wedges, if desired, and enjoy!

SERVINGS: 4 (1 quesadilla per serving)

38

Do Not Fear

God is our refuge and strength,
A very present help in trouble.
Therefore we will not fear.

—PSALM 46:1-2 NASB

Maybe you've heard this acronym for *fear*: False Evidence Appearing Real.

One reason we find ourselves fearful is that we don't know what lies ahead or how a given situation will turn out. Fear can often result from not feeling in control of the outcome of a situation. But if we stop to think about it, fearing and fretting don't help the situation or change the outcome. The way out of fear is to remember who is in control: God.

God says in His Word that He is our help. He is our strength. He is our refuge, our shelter, and our protection. When we focus our attention on the fact that God is on our side, we find our hope increasing and our fear diminishing.

The Bible says that "God has not given us a spirit of fear and timidity, but of power, love, and self-discipline" (2 Timothy 1:7 NLT). Knowing who is on our side and knowing His love for us will cast out fear (1 John 4:18). The emotion of fear can grip us and hold us back from fully living the life that God intends us to live.

So go ahead and release control of your day, of your life, and of your fear to the One who controls *all* things for your good.

> **Lord, thank You** that because I'm Yours, I need not fear. I know that fear means the enemy is trying to keep me from moving forward with You. But since I know Your love, fear has no place in my life. Help me release all fear and trust You more, Lord. In Jesus' name, amen.

39

You Are Never Alone

Be strong and courageous. Do not be afraid or terrified because of them, for the Lord your God goes with you; he will never leave you nor forsake you.
—DEUTERONOMY 31:6

One of the most wonderful promises in Scripture—and it appears in both the Old Testament and the New Testament—is God's promise that He will never leave us, and His Holy Spirit is key to God keeping this promise.

After Jesus' crucifixion and His resurrection and before He returned to the Father, Jesus promised to leave us a Comforter, Counselor, and Teacher who would be with us to guide us through this life. That Helper is the Holy Spirit (John 14:16–17). We see in the Bible that the Holy Spirit was given to us to help us in all things (1 Corinthians 2:7–16). This means that in every life situation we can go to the Lord and ask Him for direction, guidance, and help . We can also be sure that if we need to be comforted, encouraged, or reminded of the truth of God's Word, the Holy Spirit will be there both to meet that need and to remind us of the promises of Scripture that we have stored in our hearts (John 14:26).

If you are feeling worn out or burdened, if you need any kind of help today, the Holy Spirit is waiting to assist you. All you have to do is ask (Luke 11:13). You can be confident that it is His will to help you, teach you the right way to go, and provide for you, whatever you are facing (John 16:13). Nothing is too big and nothing is too small for you to pray about or for the Spirit to be involved in. You can go to the Lord about anything, for He cares deeply about you. And because He created you, He knows exactly what you need (Psalm 139:13)! Be encouraged today, for you are never alone and you are never without help!

What is an area of your life where you feel that you need help? I encourage you to take that concern to the Lord today; He is willing and able to comfort, guide, and direct you!

> **Lord, thank You** for sending the Holy Spirit to be my Comforter, my Counselor, my Teacher. When I feel alone, thank You for reminding me that You will never leave me or forsake me! Thank You, Lord, for caring enough about me that You sent Your Spirit to guide me through this life. In Jesus' name, amen.

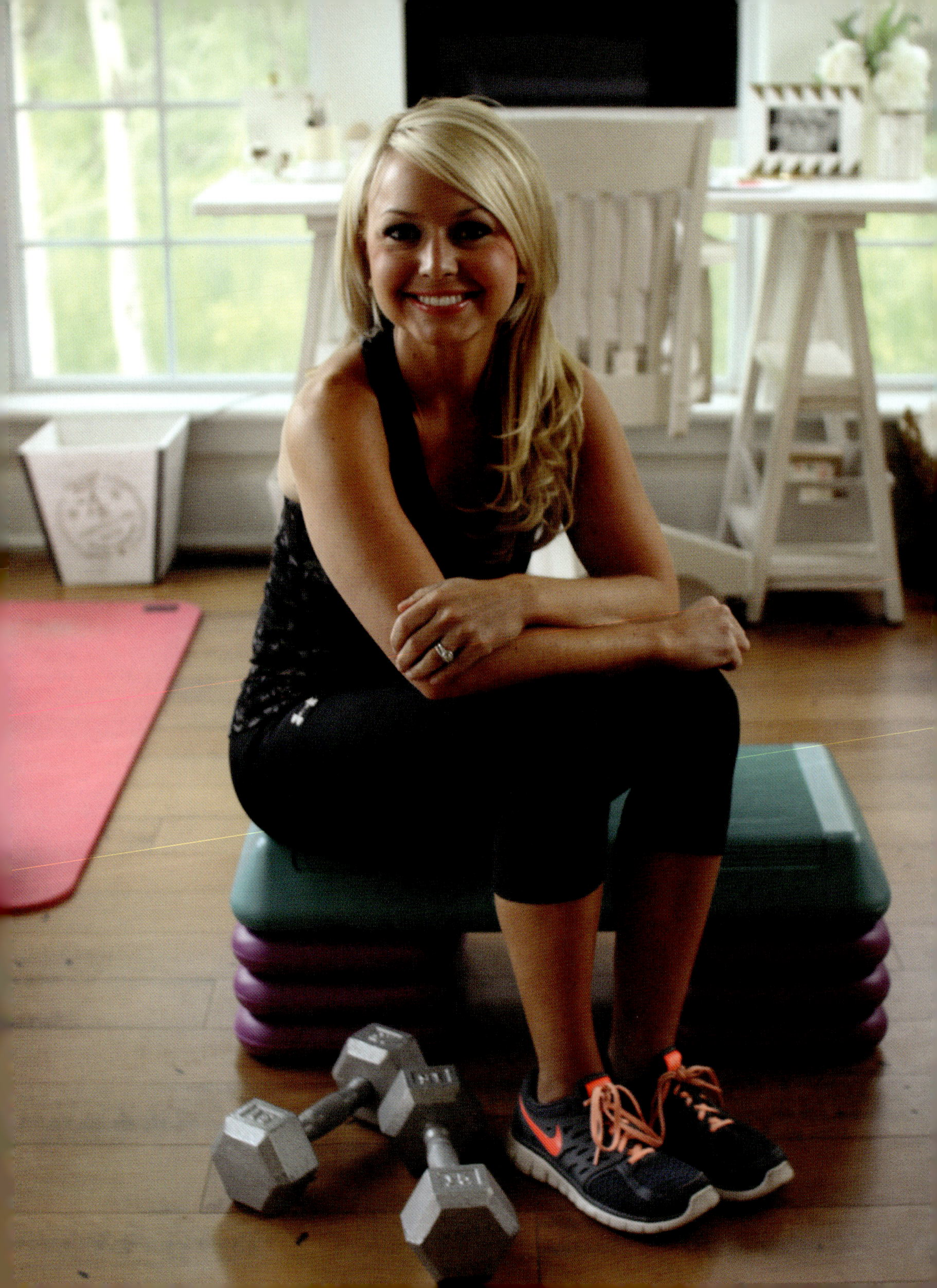

40

Free from Guilt

Adam's sin led to condemnation, but God's free gift leads to our being made right with God, even though we are guilty of many sins.
—ROMANS 5:16 NLT

If you are feeling condemned or guilty about a sin you have committed and have already confessed to God, that feeling is not from the Lord! Even though we may feel that we deserve to feel guilty at times, Jesus died so that we would not get the punishment we deserve. In fact, we clearly see in this verse that condemnation is tied to Adam's sin. Because Jesus died to redeem us from sin, we are now under the covenant of grace and are completely forgiven.

Our right standing with God—our righteousness—is a free gift from God to us. God offered His Son, Jesus, as a sacrifice for our sins, a gift of forgiveness extended to us even in the midst of our sins. We will never deserve or earn a right standing with God. Instead, we must humbly receive by faith the gift God is offering us and believe that we are right before our holy God only because of what Jesus did.

Thank You, Jesus, for the gift of righteousness—offered free to me after costing You Your life. Almighty God, when I am tempted to walk around feeling condemned because of my sinfulness, help me remember that even in the midst of my sins, You have made me right with You. Thank You, Jesus! In Jesus' name, amen.

41

Stop the Comparison Game

Pay careful attention to your own work, for then you will get the satisfaction of a job well done, and you won't need to compare yourself to anyone else.
—GALATIANS 6:4 NLT

"I wish I had her hair!" "Wouldn't it be great to have full access to her closet!" "I wish I could look like her in a bathing suit."

I used to think it was natural to have thoughts like these, but I have found in God's Word many verses that warn us not to entertain such thoughts. And that warning—like every warning and command God gives—is for our good.

One reason for this warning is that God created each of us for a unique purpose: to do some specific aspect of His kingdom work that only we can do. He also created each of us to look, act, and be unique, and that uniqueness is well designed. You see, when each of us brings our one-of-a-kind set of strengths, gifts, passions, and abilities together, we form a strong and healthy body of Christ-followers (1 Corinthians 12:12).

If we are ever going to get our eyes off other people, we must choose to keep our eyes on what God has given us—the tangibles and the intangibles—and use those blessings to love Him and to love others to the best of our ability. Each time we start to compare ourselves to others, we must deliberately choose to stop those negative thoughts in their tracks and to instead remember truths and guidelines from God's Word, like Galatians 6:4.

When we redirect our thinking from our neighbors' opinions to God's unchanging truth, He will remind us of His love and the fact that He designed each of us for a unique purpose and a destiny that no one else can fulfill.

So choose to focus on the strengths God has given you, and do the best you can with what you have in your hands. When we do this, we will know the satisfaction of a job well done, and we will give God glory as we work. Doesn't that sound a whole lot better than walking around feeling jealous?

Lord, when I find myself feeling jealous or comparing myself to others, please help me remember the truth about Your love for me and reveal to me the strengths You have placed inside me. Also help me focus on the unique plan You have created for me. I trust that as I serve where You want me to serve, I will experience the satisfaction of a job well done and I will no longer need to compare myself to anyone else. In Jesus' name, amen!

Dash of Inspiration

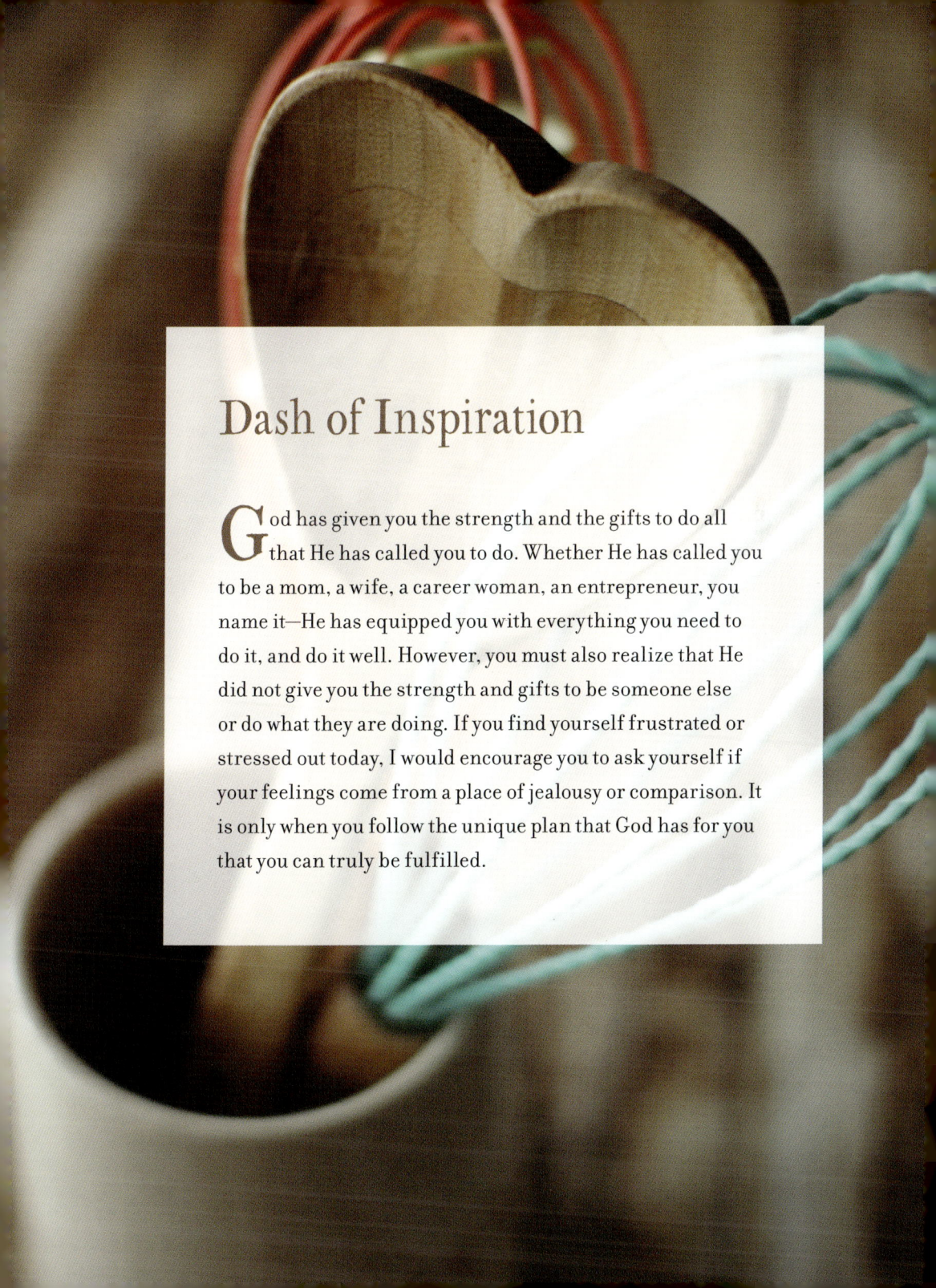

God has given you the strength and the gifts to do all that He has called you to do. Whether He has called you to be a mom, a wife, a career woman, an entrepreneur, you name it—He has equipped you with everything you need to do it, and do it well. However, you must also realize that He did not give you the strength and gifts to be someone else or do what they are doing. If you find yourself frustrated or stressed out today, I would encourage you to ask yourself if your feelings come from a place of jealousy or comparison. It is only when you follow the unique plan that God has for you that you can truly be fulfilled.

Confidence in Christ

"My grace is sufficient for you, for my power is made perfect in weakness."
—2 CORINTHIANS 12:9

If we rely on our own abilities and talents, we will most likely feel underqualified for whatever God has called us to do. Moses certainly did. We see in Exodus 3–4 that God called Moses to lead His people out of Egyptian slavery to freedom. Moses gave God excuse after excuse as to why he wasn't capable. God refuted every excuse and ended up using him mightily.

When I felt that the Lord had put it on my heart to write this devotional, there were many times I felt underqualified, but the Lord reminded me that He has given me the revelation of His Word and that the Holy Spirit would speak through me. The day I felt that way, I read Ephesians 2:10, "We are God's handiwork, created in Christ Jesus to do good works, which God prepared in advance for us to do." God gave you—His handiwork!—specific gifts, talents, and passions so that you will be able to fulfill a purpose that only you can fulfill. When you put your confidence in Christ and in His grace, you can—in His power—do all the things He calls you to do (Philippians 4:13). Remember, God knows our limitations and our shortcomings, but He sees those as opportunities to give us His strength. He sees us as vessels that He can use, but we must be willing to yield our abilities—as limited as they seem to us—to Him. He will meet us where we are and use us just the way we are.

As the Lord said to Moses, "I have raised you up for this very purpose, that I might show you my power and that my name might be proclaimed in all the earth" (Exodus 9:16).

God doesn't call the qualified; He qualifies those He calls.

> **Lord, I thank You** that Your grace is sufficient where I am insufficient, and that where I see my shortcomings, You can pour Your power into my life. I ask that You graciously supplement my talents, gifts, and abilities and use them—use me—to accomplish Your purpose for my life. In Jesus' name, amen.

Take Action!

Do not merely listen to the word, and so deceive yourselves. Do what it says.
—JAMES 1:22

Wisdom and understanding are essential tools for living a life that honors and glorifies God. His Word gives clear wisdom and direction, but if we don't apply what we learn, we can end up confused and misled, living our way, not the Lord's way. The solution is to put the spiritual truths of God's Word into action in our daily lives. In order to gain wisdom in any area of our lives, we must begin by renewing our minds with the truth of God's Word. In the area of our health, for example, we must renew our minds by learning what God says about taking care of our bodies. Then we must put this wisdom into practice, letting it guide the food we eat and the exercise routines we establish. True blessings come when we gain wisdom from God's Word and then apply it to our everyday lives! Allow the Lord to give you wisdom from above and learn to do things His way, not the way of this world.

Lord, I thank You that I will gain understanding and wisdom when I read Your Word. Please help me take the truths You show me and apply them to every area of my life. I thank You in advance for helping me find guidance and strength for healthier eating and exercising. In Jesus' name, amen.

Personal Pan Egg White Pizza

INGREDIENTS:
2 cups cauliflower and broccoli, chopped into bite-size pieces
6 large egg whites (or 1¼ cup egg whites from carton)
½ small tomato, cut into thin slices (I like Roma tomatoes for this)
Pinch of salt and pepper
1½ tablespoons Parmesan cheese, grated (or cheese of choice)
Ketchup

METHOD:
1. Start by steaming your veggies until tender. You can do this by steaming them in the microwave for 3 to 5 minutes, or until tender, either in a bowl with ¼ to ½ cup water, covered with plastic wrap and pierced with holes, or buy the steamable frozen bags of veggies). Or you could lightly sauté the veggies in a large skillet until tender.
2. Preheat oven to 425 degrees. Spray a medium nonstick skillet with cooking spray. Pour egg whites into skillet, and place steamed vegetables, tomato slices, salt and pepper, and Parmesan cheese over the top of the egg whites. Drizzle ketchup evenly over the top, if desired (this becomes like the tomato sauce in a pizza). Place skillet in the oven for 20 to 25 minutes, or until the top becomes lightly golden brown (this may vary slightly based on the size of your skillet, but the egg whites should be firm to the touch). Remove from the oven, and slide the pizza onto a plate. Cut into pizza slices, if desired, and enjoy!

SERVINGS: 1 (1 egg white pizza per serving)

119

44

Forgiving Yourself

Let us go right into the presence of God with sincere hearts fully trusting him. For our guilty consciences have been sprinkled with Christ's blood to make us clean, and our bodies have been washed with pure water.
—HEBREWS 10:22 NLT

I am pretty sure all of us have found ourselves in the place where we know God forgives us, but we just can't forgive ourselves. We feel guilty and we condemn ourselves for all the ways we have failed to be the people God wants us to be. We may even find ourselves going to God over and over, asking Him to forgive us for the same sin. The Bible says when we repent and turn to the Lord, God forgives our sins (Acts 3:19). When we hold on to our past sins, we are saying that what Jesus did on the cross wasn't sufficient enough for us to be forgiven.

Jesus knew we would all fall short of the holiness God requires of those who would enter His presence, yet Jesus died for us when we were sinners (Romans 5:8). Jesus died to set us free from the punishment for our sins—eternal separation from our holy God—and He remembers our sins no more (Hebrews 8:12). "As far as the east is from the west," so far are our sins removed from us (Psalm 103:12). Since Jesus remembers our sins no more, why should we continue to beat ourselves up for those same sins? Jesus took the beatings for our sins so that we could be free from that punishment. We are to repent of our sins, receive God's forgiveness, and then remember those sins no more. When we know God's true forgiveness, we are to forgive ourselves and leave our sins at the foot of the cross.

> **Lord, I thank You** that You died for me while I was yet a sinner. I thank You for Your forgiveness and for remembering my sins no more. Enable me, I pray, to see myself the way You see me—as forgiven and cleansed of my unrighteousness. Enable me to forgive myself. In Jesus' name, amen.

45

Perfect Peace

> You will keep in perfect peace
>   all who trust in you,
>   all whose thoughts are fixed on you!
> —ISAIAH 26:3 NLT

Perfect peace? What a wonderful promise! We have the ability to know God's perfect peace regardless of our circumstances. How are we able to have peace even in bad situations? Isaiah 26:3 shows that we experience God's perfect peace when we choose to do two things. First, we must choose to trust God. Think about it: if you trust someone to take care of you, provide for you, and guide you, to take care of what you can't take care of, then you would suddenly feel the lifting of a huge burden. Second, we choose to fix our thoughts on Him. We do this by focusing our attention on the Word of God. We must also choose to reject any thought or emotion that violates God's Word; we must align our thoughts and emotions with what God's Word says about His love, His faithfulness, His sovereignty—as well as what His Word says about us.

Then, as we trust God and fix our mind on His promises to us, we will be able to walk through life with His perfect peace.

Lord, when I am feeling anything but peaceful, I pray that You will remind me to trust in You, to reflect on Your faithfulness, and to fix my mind on Your promises. I thank You for this perfect peace that transcends circumstances and that can only be found in You. In Jesus' name, amen.

46

Experience God's Love

May you experience the love of Christ, though it is too great to understand fully. Then you will be made complete with all the fullness of life and power that comes from God.

—EPHESIANS 3:19 NLT

God's love for us is so much more than just emotion, and it is certainly greater than we could ever understand with our limited human ability. One reason we struggle to understand God's love is because the world's concept of love is too often based on performance. Our society also teaches that someone is worthy of love if they are first kind and loving to us. However, God does not love us based on our performance or our kindness. He loves us unconditionally, because He *is* love.

So how can we more fully experience His love for us? Simply pray and ask God to reveal something of His love—to help you see and feel His presence—so that you are able to notice His presence and experience His love on a daily basis. God wants you to experience His great love so that you are able to be "complete with all of the fullness of life and power that comes from [Him]."

If we find ourselves still feeling defeated, it is possible that we are not experiencing the love of God in our lives. The good news is all we have to do is ask the Lord to reveal more of His great love for us. Your Heavenly Father longs for you to know more clearly and more surely His love for you.

> **Jesus, I pray** that You will allow me to experience more fully Your great and precious love for me. Give me, I pray, a glimpse of how deep and how wide Your love for me is. I thank You for Your life-giving and life-transforming love, shown most clearly on the cross. In Jesus' name, amen.

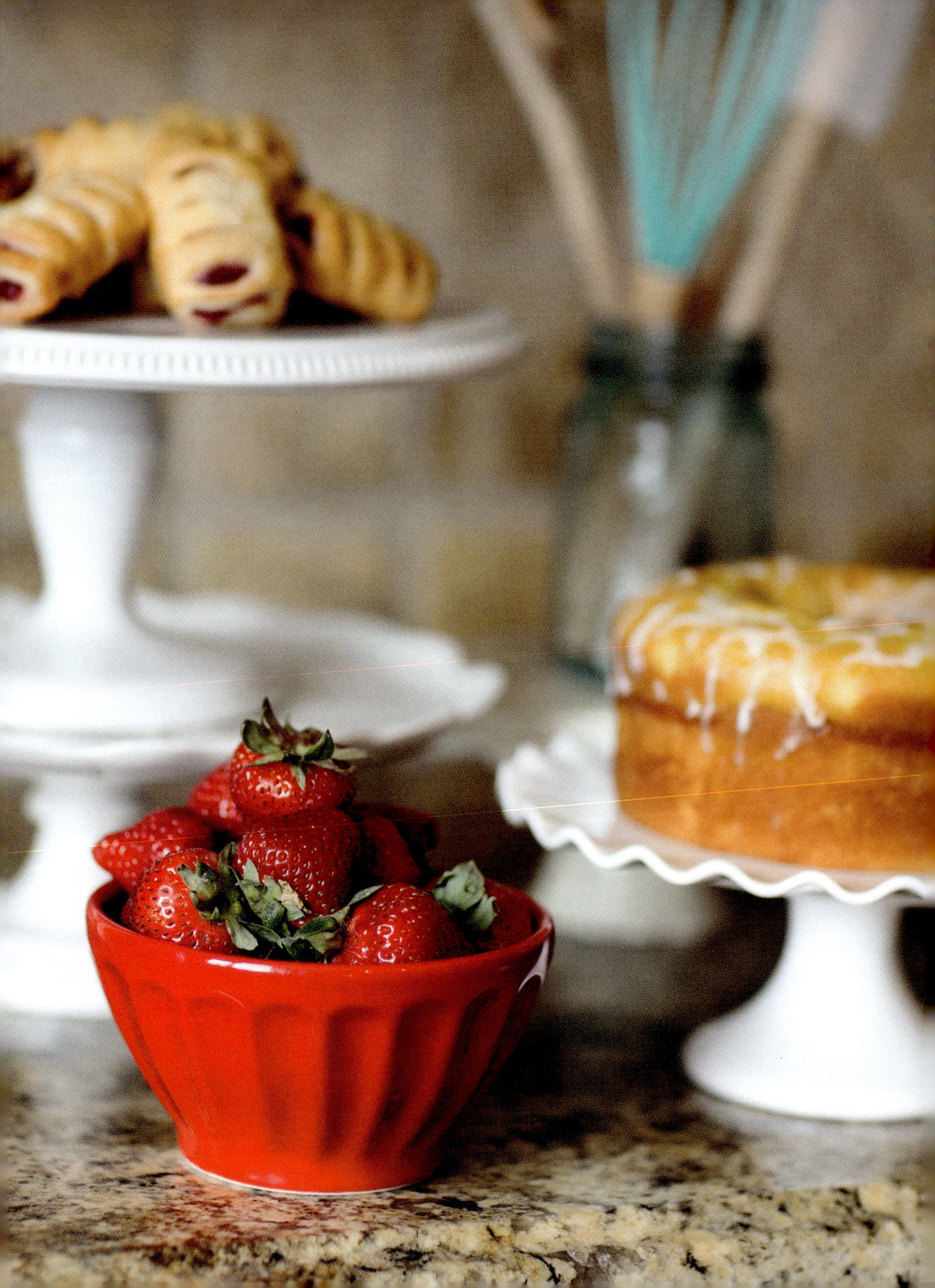

Don't Grow Weary!

Let us not grow weary while doing good, for in due season we shall reap if we do not lose heart.
—GALATIANS 6:9 NKJV

The illustration of sowing and reaping offers great encouragement whenever we are waiting for the fulfillment of one of God's promises. What an amazing portrait the Lord painted when it comes to the waiting times in our lives!

In the natural world, if we sow something, then we will get a harvest if we take proper care of the soil beforehand and proper care of the seedling once it sprouts. Part of proper care means that between the time we plant the seed and the time we see the harvest, we can't go digging up the seed to see what it's doing. A plant would never grow that way! It also means that we need to keep out of the soil any weeds that would choke and starve the seed.

Matthew 13:22 records Jesus' teaching about how the cares and worries of this life can choke the Word of God's truth sown in our hearts. We also know that worrying can stop the harvest of whatever we are trusting God for. In order to reap a harvest from the seeds of God's promises and truth, we need to plant the seed, care for the soil, and trust the Word.

After all, God can make a huge oak tree grow from one little seed. Don't grow weary while doing good, for you will reap your harvest in due season if you don't give up!

Lord, please help me find a promise in Your Word for my current situation. Help me be aware of the cares of life that will choke the word out of my heart. I will trust that You are working on my behalf and bringing forth a harvest in due season. I will not faint or grow weary in the wait, but I will trust You! In Jesus' name, amen.

48

The Importance of Prayer

Be joyful in hope, patient in affliction, faithful in prayer.
—ROMANS 12:12

Prayer is the means by which God, through you and me, advances His kingdom and His purposes here on this earth. God created us in order to be in fellowship with us. He communicates with us, grows us, equips us, prepares us, and shares His love with us when we spend time with Him.

God knows prayer is essential to a life of spiritual intimacy with Him and a source of power for all that He calls us to do. Let's get prayer off our "to-do" list for God and view it as a time when we strengthen ourselves and remind ourselves of who God is. We should never give up coming to the Lord, even when we feel like our prayers aren't being heard, much less answered—because "Not now" and "No" are answers! Those are fickle human feelings. Let's choose to believe that God hears us every time we pray and that He is delighted when we share our hearts with Him.

What does it mean to you to be faithful in prayer, as Romans 12:12 calls us to be?

Lord, please help me to be faithful and persistent in prayer, always mindful that You do hear me and that You are faithful to Your Word and faithful to Your children. I know that when I spend time with You, You enable me to be more aware of Your constant Presence with me. You also help me keep my eyes on You when the journey of life gets rough. I trust that You will give me the ability to persevere in prayer. Thank You for always being there to listen, even when I don't speak. In Jesus' name, amen!

Dash of Inspiration

I know how hard it can be to quiet your mind and spend time in prayer, especially with our busy, hectic lives. If quiet prayer time isn't currently part of your daily routine, try starting with just five or ten minutes. Go to a peaceful place you love, a favorite room or spot in the yard, and talk to God like you would a dear friend. It might just become your favorite time of day.

49

Seek and Find

"Do not seek what you should eat or what you should drink, nor have an anxious mind. For all these things the nations of the world seek after, and your Father knows that you need these things. But seek the kingdom of God, and all these things shall be added to you."
—LUKE 12:29-31 NKJV

When we look around at the world, it is clear that people everywhere are striving for things that money can buy. This hunger for the newest, latest, fastest leads to stress and anxiety as people fight not only to provide for needs, but also to purchase what they want. It is almost impossible to keep up with the newest technology when it is constantly changing. And just when we buy a new piece of clothing, we see that the newest fashion trend has hit the runway. This can end up making us feel unsatisfied and ungrateful.

If we are following Jesus, though, we are not to be like the world: striving and panicked about how to obtain what we need and want. Jesus knows that the desire to provide and care for our families and ourselves produces anxiety, so He commanded us to not seek after all the things the rest of the world is striving for. As children of God, we are instructed to seek first the kingdom of God. Doing so will mean drawing closer to the One who promises to be our Provider and Caregiver. Your heavenly Father will give you all you need.

Lord, I ask You to teach me how to seek Your kingdom first. I want to live with You as my top priority; I want to do all that I do in a way that honors and glorifies You. I thank You for Your promise to provide for my needs and my family's needs. In Jesus' name, amen.

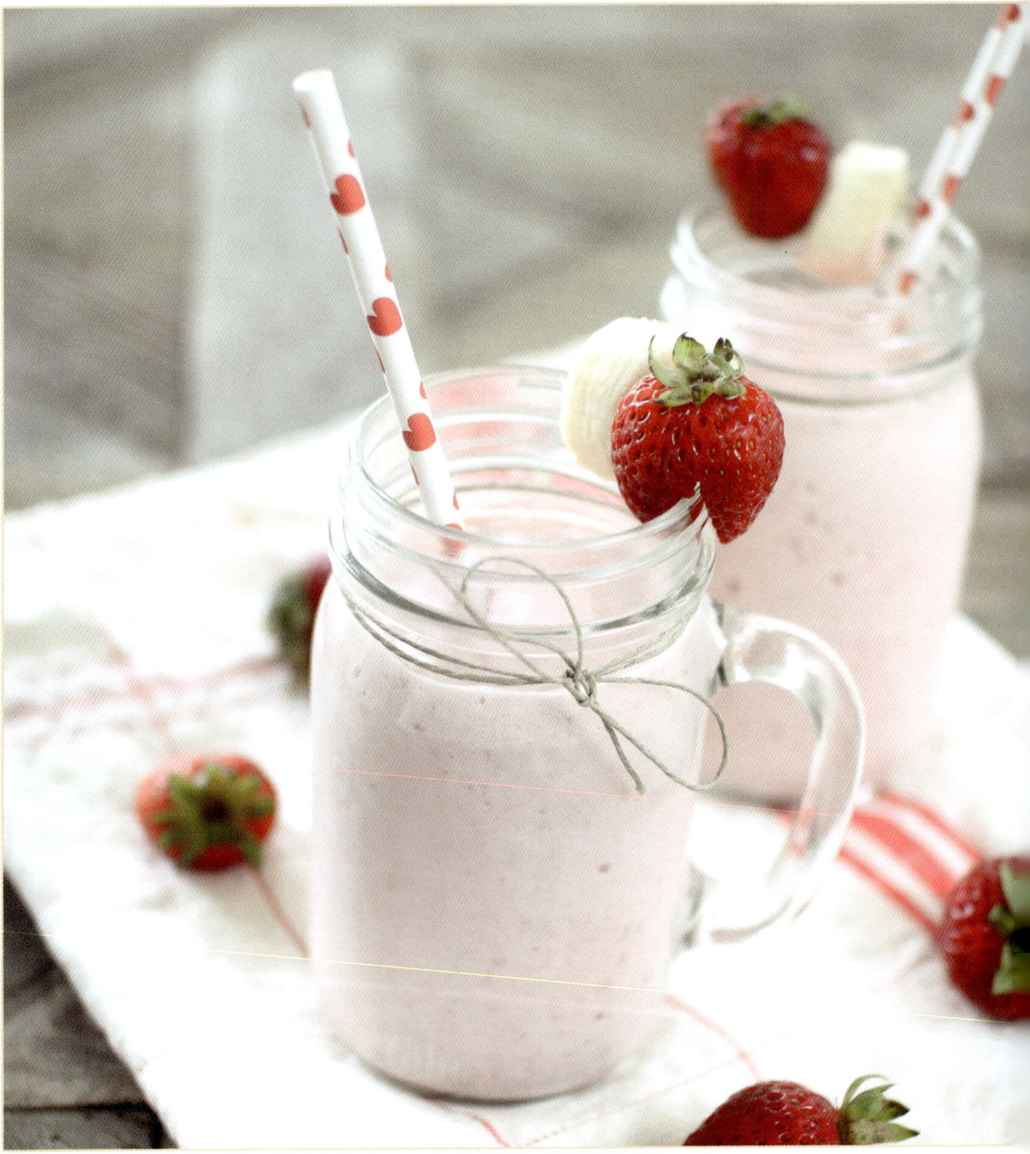

Strawberry Banana Smoothie

INGREDIENTS:
1 cup plain low-fat Greek yogurt (or low-sugar yogurt of choice)
½ cup strawberries, washed and tops removed
½ medium Banana
½–1 cup unsweetened almond milk or skim milk (adjust accordingly to desired consistency)
½–1 cup ice cubes (use less for a thinner consistency)
Optional: 1 to 3 packets stevia or 1 to 2 tbs honey (or sweetener of choice to taste)

METHOD:
1. Place all of the ingredients in a blender and blend until smooth and creamy!

SERVINGS: 1 (1 smoothie per serving)

50

Unconditional Love

Neither height nor depth, nor anything else in all creation, will be able to separate us from the love of God that is in Christ Jesus our Lord.

—ROMANS 8:39

How many times have you heard, "Jesus loves you"? More times than you can count, I'm sure. But we need to do more than just hear with our ears, more than just hold this truth in our minds. This statement must be more than a bumper sticker phrase or a cliché spoken to brighten someone's day. Each one of us needs to believe in our heart that Jesus loves us.

Consider in your heart that the very Creator of this universe calls you by name! Before you were born, the Almighty knew you (Jeremiah 1:5). After all, He knit you together in your mother's womb (Psalm 139:13), and He has a plan and purpose specifically for you (Jeremiah 29:11). The infinite and everlasting God cares about every detail of your life. He even knows the number of hairs on your head (Luke 12:7).

On certain days it's hard to believe the love that He has for us, isn't it? This can be the case for a number of reasons. Maybe something happens that makes us question if He still loves us, or maybe we simply don't *feel* His love. Although this feeling is common, we need to counter it with what our brain knows: nothing can separate us from His love. Nothing! Not emotions, not circumstances, not our actions. Nothing! I truly believe that in this lifetime we will only begin to understand the great depth, height, and length of God's love for us. The greatest act of love that has ever been or ever will be displayed is when God sent His only Son to die for you and me so we could have a close, intimate relationship with Him. Nothing can ever change the act of love He demonstrated for you and me.

Lord, I come before You and ask You to open my heart to receive Your love. I thank You that Your love for me never changes and that it's not based on my performance. And I thank You for the ultimate act of love: sending Jesus to die for me. In His name I pray, amen.

JUNE

S	M	T	W	T	F	S
1	2	3	4	5	6	7
8	9	10	11	12	13	14
15	16	17	18	19	20	21
22	23	24	25	26	27	28
29	30					

2014

51

Beauty for Ashes

The Lord has anointed me to . . .
> bind up the brokenhearted . . .
> and provide for those who grieve in Zion—

to bestow on them a crown of beauty
> instead of ashes,

the oil of joy
> instead of mourning,

and a garment of praise
> instead of a spirit of despair.

—ISAIAH 61:1, 3

Trials in life can leave our hearts feeling as if they have gone through fire. We can feel seriously wounded; our lives reduced to ashes. The good news is, no matter how shattered our lives are, God has promised to heal the brokenhearted. He promises that if we present Him with the pieces of our lives, He will give us back lives that are whole and redeemed.

At times, though, our lives may seem too broken to ever be fixed. That's when we must remember that our all-powerful God is the Creator. He created this whole earth and everything in it, so surely He can put back together the broken pieces of our lives and make something beautiful. When we trust Him with everything, He will work all things together for our good, for our growth into Christlikeness. God—for whom nothing is impossible—can bring blessing out of brokenness and replace our mourning with joy, our despair with praise.

> **Jesus, today I hand over** to You every broken piece of my life, trusting You to bring healing and restoration. Thank You in advance for taking the ashes of my life and making something beautiful, for giving me Your joy. I praise you and I pray in Your name, amen.

52

Break Every Chain

Some sat in darkness, in utter darkness,
> prisoners suffering in iron chains . . .

Then they cried to the Lord in their trouble,
> and he saved them from their distress.

He brought them out of darkness, the utter darkness,
> and broke away their chains.

Let them give thanks to the Lord for his unfailing love
> and his wonderful deeds for mankind,

for he breaks down gates of bronze
> and cuts through bars of iron.

—PSALM 107:10, 13-16

Addictions and habits that we just can't seem to shake can feel like prisons where we are chained to the very thing we want freedom from. We may even hate the thing we are doing, much like Paul described in Romans 7:18–19.

Despite the fact that we may feel like we are in a prison with no way out, we have a promise from God that He can cut through the very bars of iron that seem so strong and powerful in our lives! This passage from Psalm 107 tells us that if we cry out to the Lord in our times of trouble, He will come and rescue us out of a place of distress simply because He loves us. This passage of Scripture also reminds us that we don't need to get cleaned up before we go to God. We can be at the lowest point of our lives, at a place where we have tried hundreds of times to get free on our own and failed, and all we have to do is cry out to Him.

In His perfect timing, God Almighty will come in with His strength and break our every chain. He is able to open the door to any prison we find ourselves in and then free us to walk in the plans and purposes He has for us.

> **Lord, I ask You** to free me from _____. I have tried and failed, because I relied on my own strength. I thank You that in You I can know freedom and the fullness of joy. Lord, I choose to follow You and walk the path You have for my life. Thank You, Jesus, for setting me free! Amen!

53

Swept Clean and Filled Up

"When an impure spirit comes out of a person, it goes through arid places seeking rest and does not find it. Then it says, 'I will return to the house I left.' When it arrives, it finds the house unoccupied, swept clean and put in order. Then it goes and takes with it seven other spirits more wicked than itself, and they go in and live there. And the final condition of that person is worse than the first. That is how it will be with this wicked generation."
—MATTHEW 12:43-45

God has provided everything we need to be free from the power of Satan, but His provision does not automatically guarantee that we will walk in freedom.

When we come before the Lord and turn away—repent—from our sins, we are essentially cleaning our house. As this passage warns, though, we must not stop at repentance, for if we simply sweep our lives clean but do not fill them with anything else, they will be empty—and that can be dangerous. Empty space gives the devil room to settle in. If that happens, we can find ourselves in an even worse place than we were before.

So what do we fill our house with so that devil can't move in? That's where the Spirit of God can help. Once we have cleaned house, once we have repented of our sin, we must ask the Spirit to fill us with His truth and love, and strengthen that area of our life once dominated by sin. The filling begins when we go to God and to His Word, pouring His life-changing truth into our lives. We start when we allow the Word of God to renew our minds. The Spirit works from there to transform every area of our lives (Romans 12:2). God's Spirit will then rule in our hearts, and we are to yield to His leading and direction.

As we continue to read and study God's Word on a daily basis, we will be prepared to live according to His truth. When we are in God's Word, when we are sensitive to the presence of His Spirit within us, and when we let Jesus guide us in every area of our lives, there will not be any empty space available for the devil should he try to move back in!

Lord God, I come to You to repent of _____. I am grateful that You forgive me and wash me white as snow (Isaiah 1:18). Now, Jesus, I ask You to come and fill this and every area of my heart—every area of my life—with Your holy presence so that my life will glorify You. In Jesus' name, amen.

54

An Overcoming Faith

For everyone born of God overcomes the world. This is the victory that overcomes the world, even our faith.

—1 JOHN 5:4

As a caterpillar transforms from something that crawls and is earthbound into a butterfly that flies and soars in the sky, so are children of God transformed into overcomers. First John 5:4 explains that when we come to know Christ, we are transformed from a person who is worldly and attached to natural circumstances to a person able to rise above the circumstances of this world.

We can easily feel as if we are crawling through life. Real-life responsibilities and heartfelt concerns can keep us focused on the circumstances and the needs at hand. We can easily feel emotionally discouraged, physically drained, and spiritually dry. In a word, we can feel utterly earthbound, struggling to look up and not even thinking about flying. But like that caterpillar, you and I can know a complete transformation. After all, our Creator doesn't intend for us to crawl. He designed us to fly, but that change doesn't happen overnight.

Our faith—as the second part of this verse states—is the key to this transformation. When we put our faith in God and His promises, when we name

Jesus as our Savior and Lord, then God will enable us to do more than survive on this planet. He will enable us to overcome life's hardships by His strength and for His glory.

> **Lord, I thank You** that because I am Your child, I can know Your power that enables me to overcome the obstacles I encounter in this world. Help me expect the hard times so that when they come, I am not discouraged but instead hopeful about how You will enable me to overcome them. I know that when I put my faith in You, I set my wings in motion, and You enable me to rise above the natural circumstances of this world as I focus on You and all that will matter for eternity! Thank You, Jesus, for the work of transformation that You continue to do in me. In Jesus' name, amen!

Dash of Inspiration

From time to time I find myself giving something to God in prayer, only to find myself worrying about it again later on. Something I have been doing to help me give it to God and "leave it there" is to say out loud, "God, I trust You" whenever I find myself worrying. It has been so simple, but so profound, as it redirects my thoughts and attention back to Him, and the fact that my worries are in His hands.

When we give our burdens to the Lord, it is then that we can walk in peace in the midst of the storms of life and truly be overcomers!

55

Serving Others

Offer hospitality to one another without grumbling. Each of you should use whatever gift you have received to serve others, as faithful stewards of God's grace in its various forms.
—1 PETER 4:9-10

Have you ever had one of those days when you felt tired, overworked, stressed out, near a breaking point? And then someone—a child, a spouse, a friend, a coworker—asked you to do something! *What?!* you think. *I cannot possibly give any more of myself to anyone!* In those moments, when we feel we have nothing to give, we need Peter's reminder that when we serve others, we are truly serving the Lord. This perspective enables us to remember that when people make a request of us, we have the opportunity to use the very gifts that God has entrusted to us to minister His love to those around us.

In Matthew 25, Jesus told a parable to teach the importance of wisely using whatever time, skills, and treasure He entrusts to us. In this story three servants were given bags of gold. Two of the three invested the gold entrusted to them and gained more gold. But the third servant hid his gold in a hole, keeping it to himself. The master praised the two servants for being "faithful" with what he had given them, but he rebuked the third servant for wasting his opportunity.

If we use the time, skills, and treasure God has given us to serve others with a joyful heart, then we can be sure that He will not only call us faithful, but He will also entrust more to us (Matthew 25:23). And I don't know about you, but I long for nothing more than to hear the Lord say to me, "Well done, good and faithful servant!" (v. 21).

Let us make the choice to be found faithful by having a good attitude when we serve others!

> **Lord, I thank You** for the time, treasure, and skills You have blessed me with and entrusted to my care. Please help me use those gifts to be a blessing to people around me. May I always remember that when I am serving others, I am faithfully serving You. In Jesus' name, amen.

Crispy Popcorn Chicken

INGREDIENTS:

1 large egg

1 tbs honey (or 1 additional egg)

1 cup panko bread crumbs (or whole grain bread crumbs)

¼ cup grated Parmesan cheese

1 tsp garlic powder

1 tsp onion powder

2 tsp dried parsley

¼ tsp salt

¼ tsp pepper

1 pound boneless, skinless chicken breasts, cut into bite-size pieces

METHOD:
1. Preheat oven to 400 degrees. Spray a foil-lined baking sheet with cooking spray and set aside. In one shallow dish, whisk together egg and honey. In another shallow dish mix together panko bread crumbs, Parmesan, garlic powder, onion powder, parsley, salt, and pepper.
2. Dip chicken in egg mixture, then bread crumb mixture, and then place onto prepared baking sheet. Lightly spray chicken with nonstick cooking spray, then bake for 10 to 12 minutes, flipping halfway through so both sides are crispy. (Please note: Baking time may vary slightly based on the size of the chicken pieces and individual oven. Bake until chicken is no longer pink in the middle and is fully cooked.) Divide chicken into 4 servings, and enjoy with honey, if desired!

SERVINGS: 4 (serving size will vary slightly)

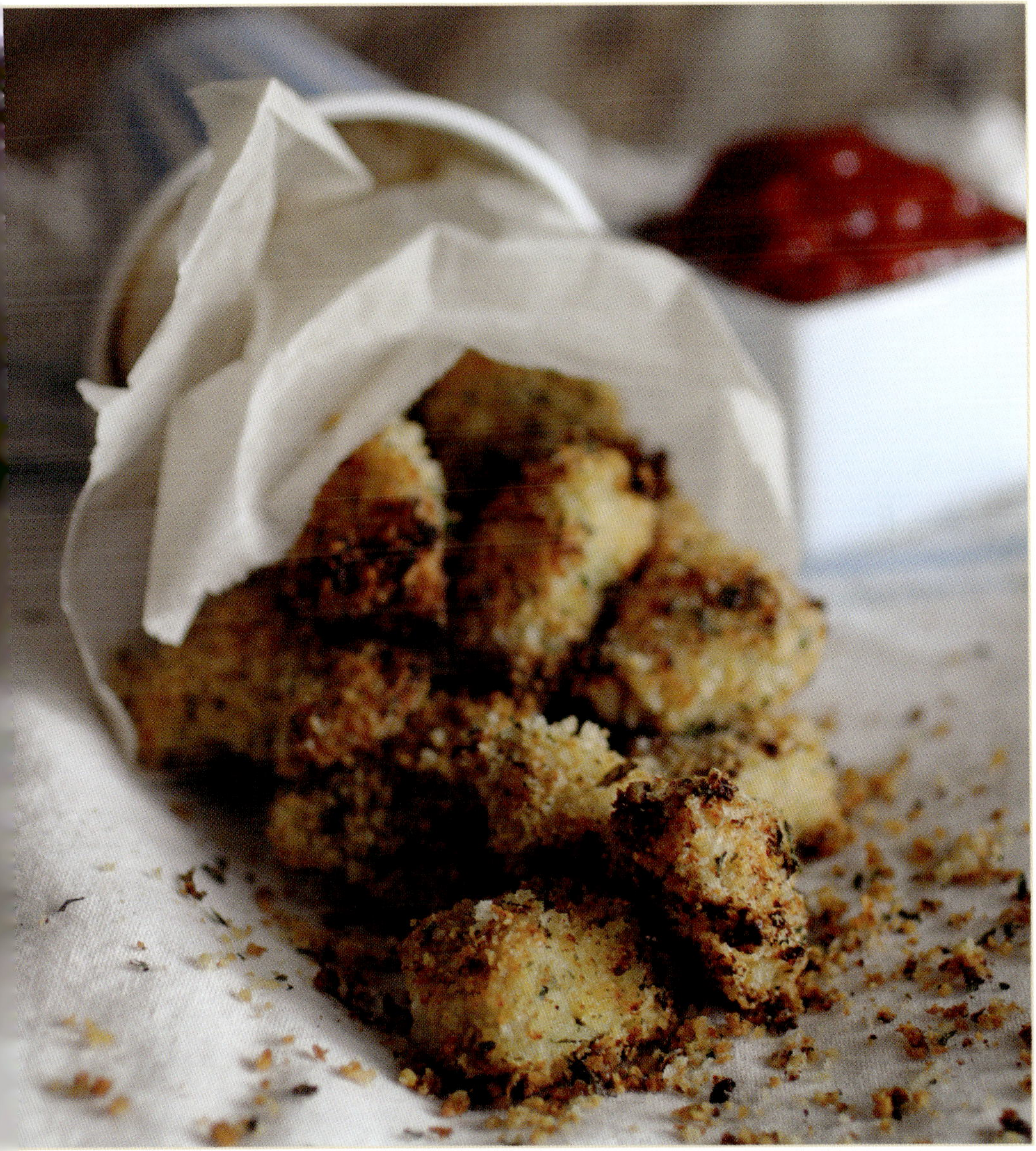

56

Growth Takes Time

Then Jesus asked, "What is the kingdom of God like? What shall I compare it to? It is like a mustard seed, which a man took and planted in his garden. It grew and became a tree, and the birds perched in its branches."
—LUKE 13:18–19

Oftentimes, when we want to make a change, we want results instantly. In today's world, it is certainly not popular or convenient to wait for anything. However, when we look at the way God created things, we should expect things to take time to grow. We would think it very strange, for instance, if we planted a seed for an apple tree and it grew overnight. God created this natural world in a way that parallels both spiritually and physically what occurs in our own lives.

If we want genuine spiritual growth, we must realize that the growth starts when we plant the Word of God in our hearts. As we protect and nourish that seed (Proverbs 4:20–27), we can be confident that the Word is growing its roots down deep into our lives and that it will eventually bring forth visible change. When we see the equivalent of a tree produced in our lives from God's Word, other people will be able to benefit from the strength and shade of that tree. Let's make the decision to begin the process of growth today. We can be sure that when we plant the seed of God's Word in our hearts, we will be like a tree, strong and immovable, and our life will be a source of refreshment to others.

Lord, today I realized that if I want to produce a constant crop of fruit for You, I need to constantly be sowing seeds of Your truth in my heart. I ask You to help me nourish the truths I plant in my heart so that my life will steadily produce life-giving fruit. In Jesus' name, amen.

57

Shine Bright

"Let your light shine before others, that they may see your good deeds and glorify your Father in heaven."

—MATTHEW 5:16

What does it mean for our light to shine before others? Jesus' words here imply an absolute truth: our lives can have a powerful and lasting impact on every person we meet. God can use everything we do and say, both little and big, to make a difference in the lives of the people around us. In fact, each one of us has been given specific gifts and talents that enable us to make an impact on someone else's life.

So many times we get caught up in thinking that we don't have anything to offer or that we have to get our own lives in order before we can bless someone else. The truth is, if we make loving God our first priority and loving others our second, then it will be impossible for us *not* to make an impact. Whether we meet someone's specific need, take a few minutes to compliment someone, listen, or even smile and say, "Hello!" to folks we see on our morning walk, God can use us to bless others. People will see our joy in the goodness of God, and they will want that for themselves. That's being a blessing!

Lord, I pray that You will help me see the people You put in my path who need some kindness or encouragement. Even if it is just in small, simple ways, use me to bless those around me. Help me shine Your light everywhere I go for all to see! In Jesus' name, amen.

58

Live to Love

Above all, love each other deeply, because love covers over a multitude of sins.

—1 PETER 4:8

When Jesus gave His life for us, hanging on that cross as penalty for our sins, He demonstrated the greatest act of love the world has ever known. No wonder Jesus calls His followers to this primary task: to love.

Love must be important because when Jesus was asked to identify the greatest commandments, He commanded His followers to love God with all we are and to love our neighbors as we love ourselves. Our love for one another is a testimony to both God's existence and His very nature, for God is love. When we walk in love for one another, our lives demonstrate that God's life-changing power is real.

Keep in mind that walking in love is easy when we are walking toward or with those who are lovely, but how do we love the unlovable? First, understand that *love* is a verb. It is not a feeling or an emotion; it is an action. That means we don't have to *feel* love for the other person, but we do need to show it. We must be obedient to God's commandment to love others regardless of our feelings.

We can begin to walk in love today by asking God to help us see others through

His eyes. When we are having a hard time loving someone, we can ask God to work in our minds and soften our hearts, to give us His compassion, and to cause His love to flow through us toward that person.

When we truly love others, we are called disciples or followers of Christ (John 13:35). If you know Jesus as your Savior and He is Lord of your life, the greatest way you can demonstrate the fact to the world is by loving the people around you with the love of God.

> **Lord, I thank** You that You demonstrated Your great love for me by sending Your only Son so that I could be in relationship with You. Help me see people with Your eyes and love them with Your love so that they will recognize You in me and will want to know you, too. In Jesus' name, amen.

59

Be Courageous!

Be strong and courageous. Do not be afraid or terrified because of them, for the LORD your God goes with you; he will never leave you nor forsake you.
—DEUTERONOMY 31:6

Many realities in this fallen world could easily cause us great fear and anxiety if we focused on them. Were we to give in to those thoughts, we could find ourselves overwhelmed with a sense of dread—and the Lord never intended for us, His children, to dread the future. Although at times we all feel afraid, we should never dwell on fearful thoughts or let anxious emotions control us.

God clearly knows that we will have trials in our lives that will tempt us to feel afraid, which is why He gives us so many precious promises to stand on to counter fear. When I start to feel fear come in, I like to remind myself of one of my favorite passages, which is found in the story of Joshua. When Joshua was facing circumstances that could have easily led to fear—crossing into the promised land and becoming the leader of the Israelites—God reminded him to be strong and courageous because He was with him wherever he went. This promise that God gave to Joshua is just as true for us today. Whatever situation we may face, we can rely on the powerful presence of the Lord with us to give us the strength and courage we need to get through it. There is no need for fear when we lean on the Lord.

If anxious thoughts threaten to overwhelm you today, I encourage you to find a quiet spot and focus your mind on the fact that the almighty God is with you at this very moment. He is mighty and powerful. He has promised to "never leave nor forsake you" (Deuteronomy 31:8). He has great plans for you, and He has promised to care for you when you cast your cares on Him (1 Peter 5:7). Rest in God's love for you today and let Him make you brave!

> **Lord, I thank You** that You are with me and that You will never leave me nor forsake me. And, Lord, because You are my Strength, my Protector, and my Provider, I can be courageous no matter what life brings. I find great strength and courage in Your presence with me! In Jesus' name, amen.

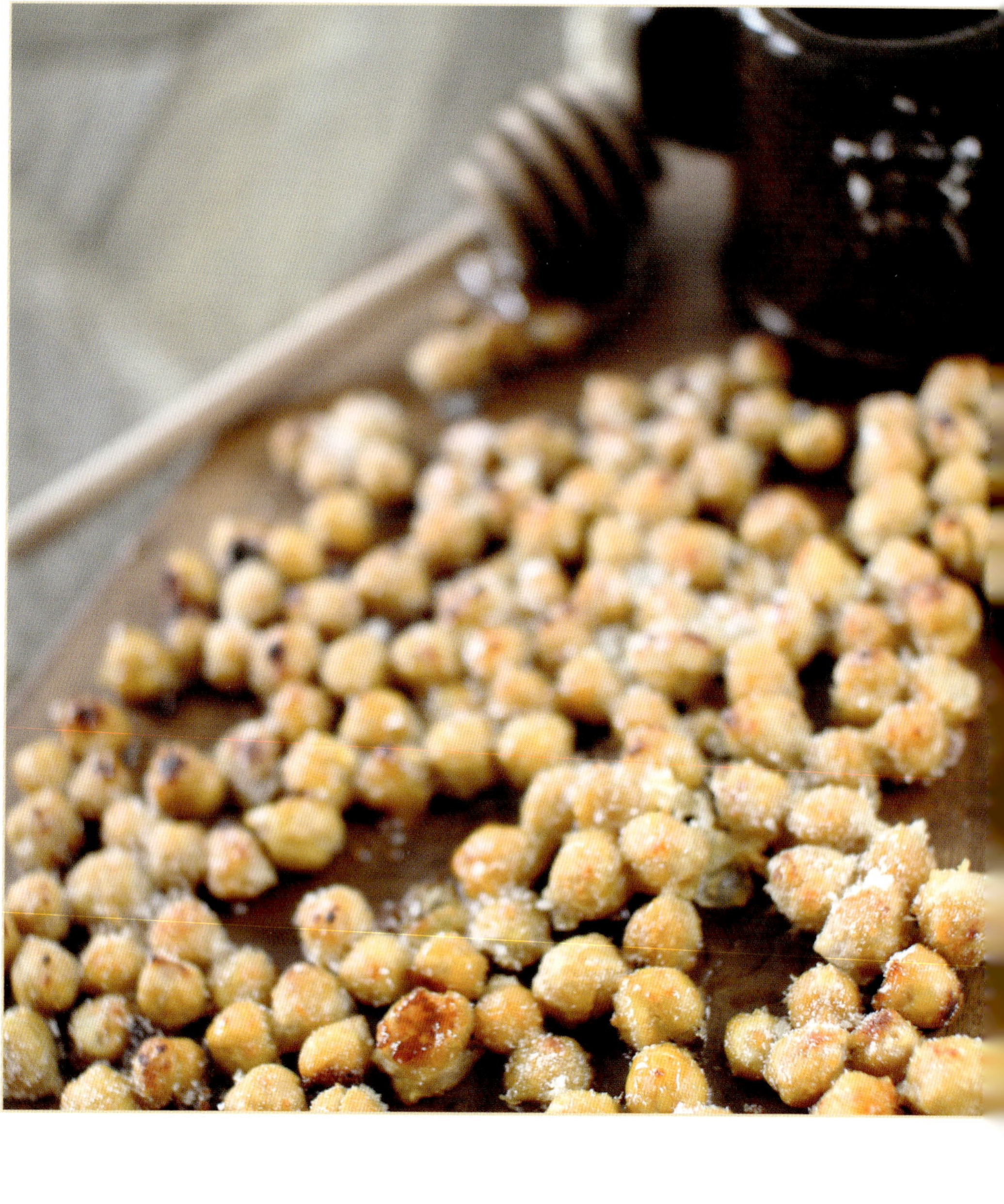

Honey Parmesan Roasted Chickpeas

INGREDIENTS:
1 (15-ounce) can chickpeas (garbanzo beans)
¼ tsp garlic powder
½ tsp salt
1-2 packets stevia (or 1 tbs sweetener of choice)
¼ cup grated Parmesan cheese
2 tbs honey

METHOD:
1. Drain and rinse the chickpeas. Blot dry with a paper towel (the drier you get them, the crispier they will become). Preheat oven to 425 degrees. Line a baking sheet with foil, and spray with nonstick cooking spray (or you could use parchment paper).
2. Spread the chickpeas out on a baking sheet in a single layer. In a small bowl mix together the garlic powder, salt, sweetener, and Parmesan cheese. Sprinkle mixture evenly over chickpeas on baking sheet.
3. Bake the chickpeas for 15 to 20 minutes, until they look slightly crispy. Remove from the oven and drizzle honey over the chickpeas. Return to oven for an additional 5-10 minutes, or until chickpeas are lightly golden brown. Let cool and enjoy! (Note: These can be stored in the fridge for up to 1 week.)

SERVINGS: 4 (about ¼ cup per serving)

60

The Power of Obedience

Just as through the disobedience of the one man the many were made sinners, so also through the obedience of the one man the many will be made righteous.
—ROMANS 5:19

Throughout Scripture we read accounts of how people's obedience and disobedience affected not only their own lives but often an entire nation. The greatest example of this is Jesus Himself: Christ's obedience to death on the cross made a way for us to be called children of God. Likewise, our choices can have a lasting impact on both our own lives and the lives of the people around us.

God has specific plans laid out for each one of us, and He promises to complete the good work that He has begun in us (Philippians 1:6), but we have a part to play. When we follow God, He will guide us every step of the way. Each step He tells us to take—or not take—is an important step toward the fulfillment of His good plan. When we obediently take the next step, God releases His power into our lives.

Another reason that obedience to God is important is because our choices will not only impact our own lives, but they could also have a lasting impact on generations to come. Just look at the story of Adam and Eve, for example. They made one poor choice and disobeyed God, and the world as God originally created it was forever changed. On the flip side, good choices can also affect generations to come. If we look at Noah's choice to listen to God and build the ark, we can safely say that this wise step of obedience had lasting results. If we would stop and take a moment to think of how our choices today could impact someone decades from now, I'm sure we would be a bit more quick to obey.

So let's choose to obey God's leading each step of the way throughout our lives. We may not always be comfortable and His instructions may not always make sense to us, but we can be sure that He will bless our faith when we choose to do what He says. Obedience honors God and brings glory to His name!

Jesus, I thank You for Your ultimate act of obedience. You have given Your life so that I could be called a child of God. You are the greatest example I have of how the obedience of One can impact many! Help me follow Your example and obey Your leading in my life. In Jesus' name, amen.

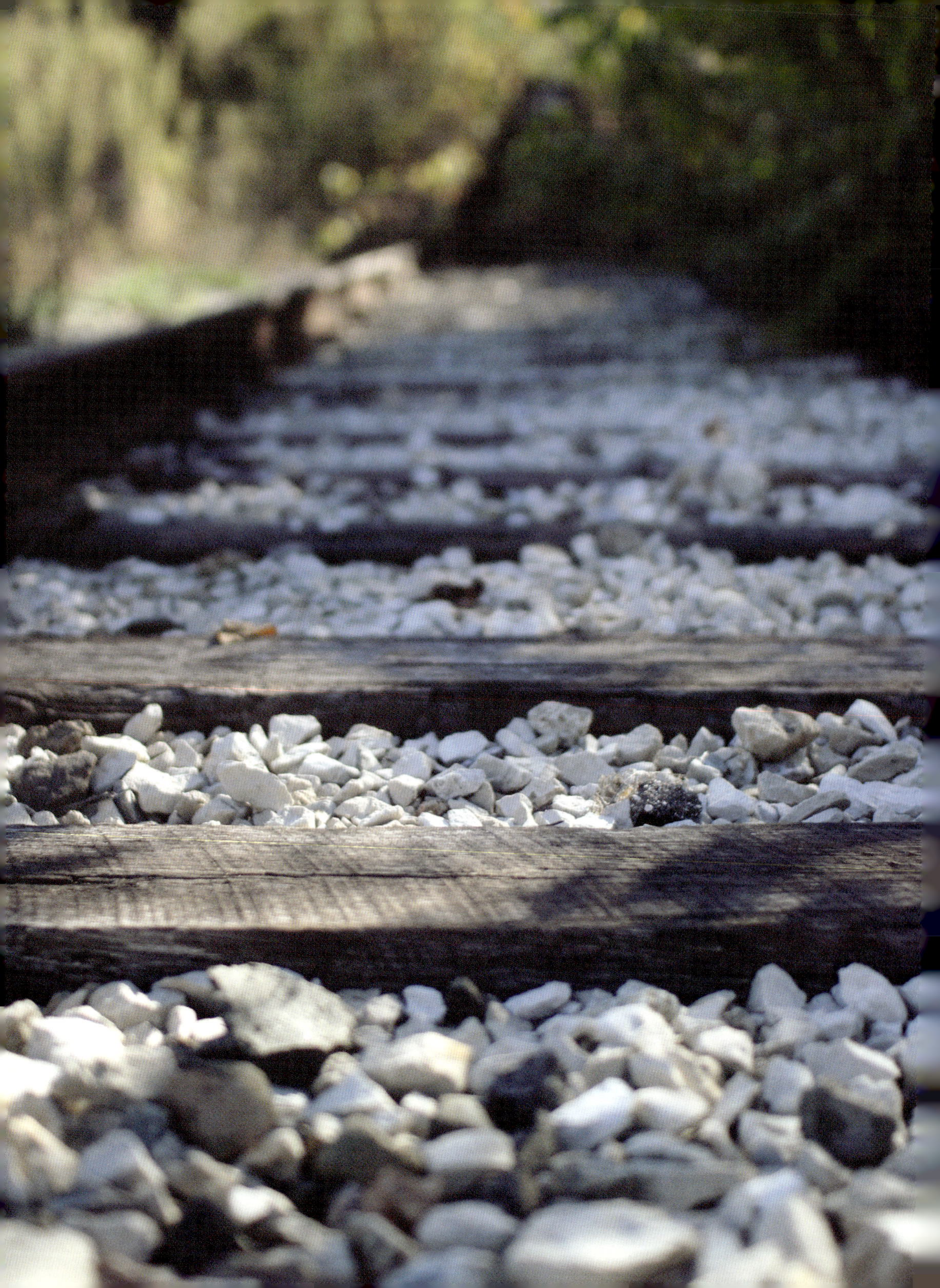

61

How to Find God's Will

I urge you, brothers and sisters, in view of God's mercy, to offer your bodies as a living sacrifice, holy and pleasing to God—this is your true and proper worship. Do not conform to the pattern of this world, but be transformed by the renewing of your mind. Then you will be able to test and approve what God's will is—his good, pleasing and perfect will.

—ROMANS 12:1-2

I will never forget seeking God during the season when I was trying to find His will for my life. I was working as a registered nurse at the time, and I started *Dashing Dish* on the side as a hobby. It wasn't long before this recipe site became much more than a creative outlet, as it also became a place where God was using me to minister to countless women about their body image, self-esteem, and identity. About two years after I started *Dashing Dish*, I felt the Lord prompting me to pursue *Dashing Dish* as a full-time ministry. It was at that time that I began to seek God's will for my life in a whole new way. I no longer wanted to follow *my* plan for my life, but rather I wanted to follow *His* plan every step of the way.

You may be facing decisions in your own life today about following God's plan for you. If that's the case, the first place to start is to recognize that God has a unique plan for your life. The Bible tells us that He has a plan for every person on this earth—and every person who has ever lived—before they are even born (Psalm 139:16). He created everything about you for a specific purpose, including when you were born, your unique abilities and talents, and your personality. Although God has a plan for each one of us, we won't fulfill that purpose unless we actively pursue it.

Once we realize that we are responsible for discovering God's will, the next step is to start seeking God. The good news is, He wants us to know His will for our lives even more than we want to find it, but He does expect us to seek Him with all our hearts in order to find His will (Jeremiah 29:12–13). The reason for this one requirement is because God loves *us* more than He loves whatever we might do for Him. For that reason, He will never lead us to do something unless we are walking with Him. The good news is, if we seek God with all of our hearts, we will find Him and His specific plan for our lives (Matthew 7:7). Seeking will require diligence on our part, but seeking God is always worth the time and effort we invest!

The next step in recognizing God's individual, personal plan for us is to realize that He will often reveal it to us in stages instead of all at once. As we step out obediently and in faith, trusting Him each step of the way and proving ourselves faithful to do what He calls us to do, He will show us the next step.

One thing we certainly can be sure of is that our heavenly Father wants us to walk in obedience to Him in every area of our lives. For it is when we walk with God that we can greatly impact the world around us for His glory!

Lord, I thank You for the wonderful plan You have for my life! I pray that You will help me consistently and diligently seek Your will about your plan for me. I thank You that You will be faithful to show me where to go every step of the way, all for Your glory. In Jesus' name, amen.

62

You Are Precious to God

How precious to me are your thoughts [about me], God!
How vast is the sum of them!
—PSALM 139:17

What a miracle that the Creator of this universe thinks about you and me. And not only a few thoughts here and there, but a vast sum! He cherishes us so much that He has us on His mind and on His heart constantly, all the time, 24-7. You and I are His children, unique and special in every way. How wonderful it would be if we could see ourselves from His point of view, the perspective of a devoted Father who let His only Son die on the cross so that you could be with Him. You are valuable. You in your finiteness, you with your limitations, you who are made of dust—you are valuable to the infinite, the unlimited, the eternal God. If you ever doubt that truth, read it in black and white. Whenever you are tempted to feel unimportant or unworthy or unlovable, simply open your Bible to Psalm 139. Let these words speak to you of the intimacy of God's love for you. He treasures you!

You created my inmost being;
    you knit me together in my mother's womb.
I praise you because I am fearfully and wonderfully made;
    your works are wonderful,
    I know that full well.
My frame was not hidden from you
    when I was made in the secret place,
    when I was woven together in the depths of the earth.
Your eyes saw my unformed body;
    all the days ordained for me were written in your book
    before one of them came to be.
How precious to me are your thoughts, God!
    How vast is the sum of them! (Psalm 139:13–17)

Lord, I thank You that I am "fearfully and wonderfully made." I thank You for "knitting me together in my mother's womb," for that picture of Your intimate crafting and attention to detail. I am humbled and grateful that I am so precious to You, that You think of me all day long! Lord, please help me see that I have worth and value because I am Yours. When I feel discouraged or unimportant, I ask that You will bring these truths back to my mind. In Jesus' name, amen!

Dash of Inspiration

Do something nice for yourself today. Go for a walk, read a good book, or take a relaxing bath. Not only will this help you relax and unwind, but it will help you find joy in your every day life. Just as a good parent would want the child whom she loves to laugh, smile, and enjoy each day, our Heavenly Father wants that for each one of His children as well!

Are You Running on Empty?

He gives strength to the weary
 and increases the power of the weak.
—ISAIAH 40:29

None of us thinks we have enough of it. We all wish we had more. What am I talking about? Time.

Time is actually a more valuable resource than money. Unlike other resources, it is the one thing we can't create more of. And since we can't create more time, we humans try to stretch it: we fill our hours and our days, often beyond what we can handle. God never designed our physical bodies or our spirits to constantly run at such a fast pace without ever resting. That's why we may suddenly crash emotionally, physically, or spiritually.

After all, when we try to do it all, we are neglecting something very important: we're neglecting ourselves. We're not taking good care of ourselves. We are running on empty and are no longer able to give anything significant to any person or any effort. If we will slow down, learn to say no, and prioritize, God will bless our balanced life and enable us to give our best to whomever and whatever He puts in our path.

When we're running—and running fast—often the first thing to go is our time with the Lord. We think, *If only I had more time, I would spend time with the Lord.* The problem is, if we don't run to Him first and put Him first, other aspects of our lives *will* falter. The Lord is our Source of energy and strength.

Most of us are very good about charging our phones daily so that they don't run out of juice, but we don't treat our lives as well as we treat our phones. We must spend time with the One who will recharge us, give us strength, guide our steps, keep us from growing weary, and help us throughout our day. Remember, it is important to take a break, to take time for yourself, to recharge. It is essential that we put the Lord first and make Him the top priority of every day. Besides being wise and healthy, when we spend time with the Lord, we can accomplish more than what we would on our own.

> **Lord, thank You** for allowing me to recognize when I'm running too fast. Help me take time for myself, give me the strength to say no, and provide me wisdom for prioritizing my day. Above all else, help me be disciplined about carving out time for You so that You can equip me for the day ahead. In Jesus' name, amen.

Lemon Blueberry Pancakes

INGREDIENTS:
½ cup oat flour (or ¾ cup old-fashioned oats ground into flour)
1 tsp baking powder
½ tsp baking soda
¼ cup protein powder (or additional oat flour)
2 to 4 packets stevia (or 1 to 2 tbs sweetener of choice, or to taste)
⅓ cup plain low-fat Greek yogurt
2 large (⅓ cup) egg whites
2 tbs lemon juice
½ cup fresh blueberries
Optional: zest of one lemon

METHOD:
1. In a medium bowl mix together the oat flour, baking powder, baking soda, protein powder, and stevia. Add the yogurt, egg whites, and lemon juice and mix well. Gently fold in the blueberries and lemon zest, if desired.
2. Preheat skillet on medium heat. Spray with nonstick cooking spray and pour the batter into the skillet (2 to 3 tablespoons for a medium pancake and ¼ cup for a larger one). Cook for a couple minutes until you see the edges turning brown and bubbles start to form on the top. Flip with a spatula and cook until browned on the other side. Enjoy!

SERVINGS: 2 (serving size will vary slightly)

173

64

Praying the Word of God

*"If you abide in Me, and My words abide in you, you will
ask what you desire, and it shall be done for you."*
—JOHN 15:7 NKJV

One of the biggest lies Christians believe is a lie about our prayer life. Many Christians believe that prayer is meant to convince God to do something. It may be easy to grasp that God is all-powerful and can do anything, but it may be quite difficult to believe that He truly cares enough about us and our concerns to answer our prayers. Maybe if we are good enough, if we pray long enough, or if we are persuasive enough, then He will answer our prayers. This perspective on prayer is far removed from biblical truth.

Rather than pleading with God, we can go to God in prayer, knowing that if we ask anything according to His will (which is revealed in His Word), He hears us (1 John 5:14). One way to be sure that we are praying the perfect will of God is to pray scripturally based prayers. Scripture—with its estimated three thousand promises—*is* the perfect will of God. So when we pray the Word, we know that we are praying His will be done; we know that His answer to that prayer will be yes and amen. Second Corinthians 1:20 says, "All of God's promises have been fulfilled in Christ with a resounding 'Yes!' And through Christ, our 'Amen' (which means 'Yes') ascends to God for his glory" (NLT). So rather than praying and waiting to see if our prayers will be answered, we can pray the Word, knowing that what we request in God's name and in His own words is a done deal. Such confident prayer means a thankful heart: we know we are declaring God's truth over our situation. Prayer is a way we commune with the Lord, but it can also be a way we encourage ourselves with the promises of God.

How can you pray confidently today, speaking the Word of God with faith?

Lord, thank You for Your Word, a roadmap revealing Your perfect will. Thank You that because I am righteous in Christ, I can come boldly before You in prayer. Please transform my prayer life. Help me find scriptures that give me words—Your words—for situations I face. In Jesus' name, amen.

65

Learning to Wait

Wait on the LORD;
Be of good courage,
And He shall strengthen your heart.
—PSALM 27:14 NKJV

*P*atience and *waiting* are words that most of us dislike. After all, in our fast-paced society, we like to get things—and get them *fast*. So when we approach God in prayer, we often come expecting the same kind of quick results. We look for immediate answers, and when they don't come, we tend to get frustrated, lose heart, or, even worse, stop praying about that issue.

Our God is almighty and all-powerful. He could answer prayers immediately, but often He chooses to grow our faith and develop our perseverance. James 1:2–4 says, "Consider it pure joy, my brothers and sisters, whenever you face trials of many kinds, because you know that the testing of your faith produces perseverance. Let perseverance finish its work so that you may be mature and complete, not lacking anything." God wants His children to be mature in their faith. So when we don't see our prayers answered immediately, we are not to lose heart. We have to remember that God's timing is perfect. He knows the end and the beginning (Isaiah 46:10), and He knows what is best for us.

Proverbs 3:5–6 says, "Lean on, trust in, and be confident in the Lord with all your heart and mind and do not rely on your own insight or understanding. In all your ways know, recognize, and acknowledge Him, and He will direct and make straight and plain your paths" (AMP). We are not to figure out or dictate to God the plan for our lives. Instead, we are to trust Him, the One who designed the perfect plan for us before we were born. Besides, some of the greatest life lessons happen as a result of delayed gratification. When we do receive what we have been praying about and waiting for, those answered prayers are some of life's most treasured blessings.

> **Lord, sometimes I don't understand** Your timing, but I know that You have Your hand upon me and will never leave me. So as I wait, please strengthen my heart and calm my emotions. Help me find joy in the waiting and joy in the fact that You are growing and maturing me. In Jesus' name, amen.

66

Praying for Yourself

Is anyone among you in trouble? Let them pray.

—JAMES 5:13

If you're in trouble, pray.

So often we run to other people and say, "Will you please pray for me?" That's a good thing, but it's not the only thing, and maybe it's not the best *first* thing to do. Of course there is nothing wrong with asking people to pray for us or joining with others in prayer. But it is also good to be comfortable praying by ourselves for ourselves. In other words, we need to readily run to the One who created us and knows us, who is the Author of all history and of our personal histories, who has infinite power and wisdom and already knows the beginning and the end of the story.

When we discipline ourselves to turn to God, to search His Word for guidance and hope, and to spend time in prayer by ourselves, He will bless us by strengthening our faith and equipping us for the future. Carving out time, finding quiet moments, and learning to hear God's voice will be well worth it.

What situation might you take to God privately now? Journal your experience as you move forward.

Lord, I thank You that I can always come to You. Help me develop that spiritually healthy habit of running to You. Enable me to be disciplined about spending quiet time with You. I trust that as I seek You, I will find You, and when I pray to You, I'll hear Your voice. In Jesus' name, amen.

67

Hearing God's Voice

Your ears shall hear a word behind you, saying,
"This is the way, walk in it,"
Whenever you turn to the right hand
Or whenever you turn to the left.

—ISAIAH 30:21 NKJV

God created us to be in fellowship with Him; He wants to speak to us, and He wants us to speak to Him as well.

And there is more good news: we can hear His voice! John 10:27 says, "My sheep hear My voice, and I know them, and they follow Me" (NKJV). Most people assume God isn't speaking if they don't hear an audible voice. Although God can and does speak to people audibly, He usually uses "a still small voice" (1 Kings 19:12 NKJV), a voice that can easily and often be mistaken as our own thoughts. How can we tell the difference?

We can distinguish God's voice from our personal thoughts because His voice will offer peace, comfort, and wisdom. His voice will always lead us to truth. But there is another voice that will try to compete with the Lord's voice, and that would be the enemy's voice. We can discern it as the voice of Satan because it brings confusion, deception, doubt about God's Word, and fear. Also competing for our attention is the voice of our flesh. Like a young, untrained, and undisciplined child, our flesh simply and selfishly demands whatever it wants.

So how do we tune out other voices and learn to recognize God's voice? By spending time with the Lord and by learning to know His heart. Hear one of God's promises: "You will call upon Me and go and pray to Me, and I will listen to you. And you will seek Me and find Me, when you search for Me with all your heart" (Jeremiah 29:12–13 NKJV). Knowing the voice of God is something we will learn over time as we quiet our minds, still our bodies, and open our hearts to hear Him speak to us.

Lord, I long to learn to recognize Your voice. I want to discipline myself to regularly spend quiet time with You so I don't miss Your still, small voice. I want to know You better. I want to discover and live according to the plan You have for me. I want to follow as You guide. In Jesus' name, amen.

68

While You're Waiting

Why are you cast down, O my inner self? And why should you moan over me and be disquieted within me? Hope in God and wait expectantly for Him, for I shall yet praise Him, Who is the help of my countenance, and my God.
—PSALM 42:11 AMP

We all have times when we are praying for a breakthrough or a change in our circumstances, and yet we don't immediately see the answer. During those times, it is crucial that we choose a proper way to wait.

We have two options during a waiting period: passive waiting or expectant waiting. When we wait passively, we have an "if it happens" attitude. Passive waiting requires no commitment, effort, or energy on our part. We don't commit to praying, worshipping, or seeking the Lord on that issue. When we wait expectantly, however, we choose to believe that God is at work. We commit ourselves to prayer, worship, and seeking the Lord's guidance. We expect to see evidence of God being present with us.

The choice we make—passive waiting or expectant waiting—can determine just how long we wait and the state of well-being during the waiting period. Synonyms for the word *wait* are "anticipate" and "expect." When a woman is pregnant with a child, she anticipates the birth of her baby. During those nine months she prepares for the child's arrival and has an expectant hope. Every day her vision of holding that baby grows more real.

We can learn to wait with that mom-to-be's same sense of hope by using the imagination God has given us. As we praise the Lord for His answers to our prayers, our hope will increase. And we can approach our waiting with the image of a waiter at a restaurant. Those waiters are not idle, and we aren't to be either. Waiting on the Lord doesn't mean sitting around hoping that everything will somehow fall into place without us doing something. It is important that we cooperate with God as we wait, that we let Him use times of waiting to prepare and equip us for whatever is ahead.

May we learn to wait expectantly for God to answer our prayers, confidently anticipating that His answers will be far greater than what we would ask or even imagine (Ephesians 3:20).

Is there a situation in your life that has left you waiting? Pray expectantly now.

> **Lord, I ask** that You enable me to wait patiently and expectantly for Your answers to my prayers. Grow and mature my faith as I wait expectantly, not passively; as I wait with a heart of hope and a song of praise for the good You are doing in my life. In Jesus' name, amen.

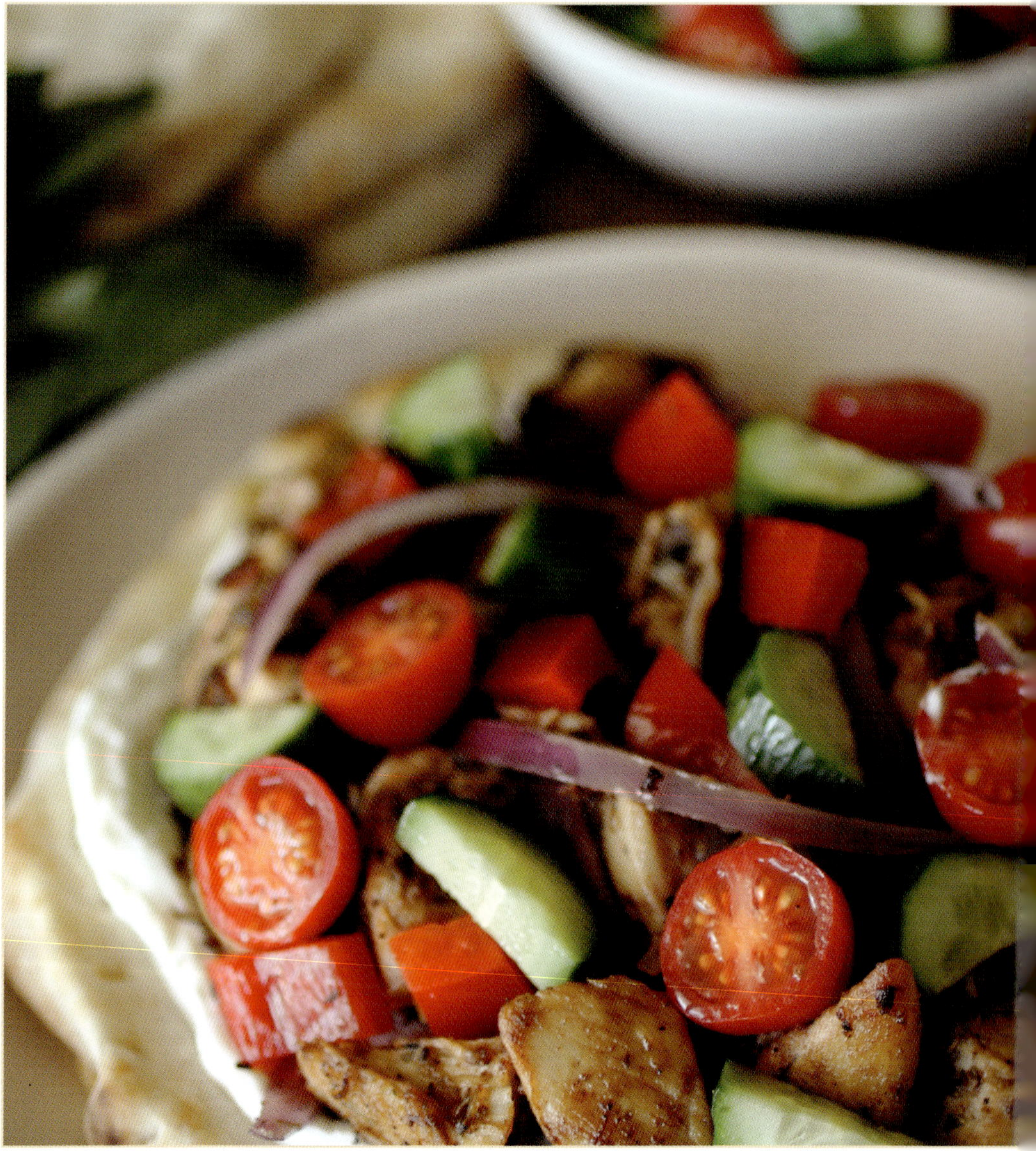

Greek Crockpot Chicken

INGREDIENTS:

½ cup chicken broth

2 tbs lemon juice

1 tbs honey

1 tbs dried oregano

1 tbs minced garlic (or 1 tsp garlic powder)

½ tsp onion powder

½ medium red onion, cut into strips

1 pound boneless, skinless chicken breasts, cut into bite-size cubes or strips

METHOD:
1. In 6-quart slow cooker, combine chicken broth, lemon juice, honey, oregano, garlic, and onion powder. Add onion and chicken, and mix to coat chicken with seasoning.
2. Cover and cook on high for 2 to 4 hours or on low for 4 to 6 hours, or until chicken is cooked through.

SERVINGS: 4 (about ½ cup cooked chicken per serving)

69

Confidence Before God

Let us then approach God's throne of grace with confidence, so that we may receive mercy and find grace to help us in our time of need.
—HEBREWS 4:16

The Lord tells us to approach His throne with confidence. Too often, however, we run from God because we don't think we are worthy to come to Him—and the truth is we aren't. We often run because of feelings of shame and guilt. The fact is that we *are* unworthy! But Jesus died on the cross for us, so now when we approach God's throne, He sees not our natural unworthiness, our shame, our guilt; He sees us "arrayed . . . in a robe of his righteousness," the righteousness of Christ (Isaiah 61:10).

God sees Jesus' finished work on the cross. Because of what Jesus did on the cross, we are now given His righteousness and are called heirs of Christ. We are not given these titles based on our actions; we are the given the righteousness of Christ when we are born again. God wants us to run to Him as He waits with open arms. We can come with confidence, knowing that He loves us and knowing that He hears us and will answer us.

The second part of that verse tells us that when we come to Him, we will receive mercy and grace for our time of need. God already knows we need help, and He is reminding us that we can receive help from the One who offers it freely.

One of my favorite things to do is to imagine myself as a little girl running into the arms of my Daddy, God. I picture Him standing with His arms outstretched with the biggest smile on His face. One of the most important things we can do is envision Him as an approachable, loving Father. His arms are always open and outstretched, waiting for us to run to Him.

> **Jesus, because You paid** the penalty for my sin on the cross, I am now a new creation. Thank You! I thank You, Father, for reminding me that You accept me and love me even though I am far from perfect. Help me see myself as You see me, and help me have confidence to run to You at all times. In Jesus' name, amen!

Dash of Inspiration

Think of the person you love most in the entire world. Think of how big your love for that person is. Now try to imagine how much bigger God's love is!

70

Staying Hungry

"Blessed are those who hunger and thirst for righteousness,
 for they will be filled."
—MATTHEW 5:6

Are you hungry? If I were talking about physical hunger, you would be able to answer that question in an instant. However, I'm not talking about physical hunger. I'm talking about being hungry for more of God. The book of Psalms tells us that God "satisfies the thirsty and fills the hungry with good things" (107:9). But in order to be filled, we must first meet one important requirement: we must be hungry.

When we first give our lives to the Lord, we experience a burning hunger to better know our newly discovered Savior. In the beginning, we may spend a great deal of time feeding our souls with His Word and fueling this newly found love that we have for Jesus. However, as time goes by, our fervor for our relationship with God can cool, much as our passion for any relationship can. We may let the busyness and cares of this life distract us and, as a result, our focus and passions can easily get redirected, or even misdirected, and our relationship with our Savior suffers.

This unfortunate situation can happen to all of us if we aren't careful. As our hearts and minds begin to get filled with the busyness of life instead of Jesus, it won't be long before we lose our hunger for Him. The main problem with this is, things other than God will ultimately and always leave us unsatisfied.

God created us to be in fellowship with Him. That's why when we aren't in close communion with Him, we inevitably feel that we are lacking something—because we are! We can try to satisfy our need for God with things in this world, but only He can truly satisfy our hearts.

If you find yourself with a loss of passion for the things of God, begin by asking yourself what happened to your appetite for Him. What have you filled your life with instead of God? If you aren't hungry for the Lord, ask Him to both show you and help you clear out the junk food that you've been filling up on—and then be sure to do your part in pursuing Him. When you choose to satisfy your appetite for God with Him and Him alone, you will indeed "taste and see that the Lord is good" (Psalm 34:8)!

> **Lord, I know** that only You can satisfy my soul, but I confess my lack of hunger for You. Please show me those things that I am filling up on other than You, and I will commit to doing my part in pursuing You today and each day for the rest of my life. In Jesus' name, amen.

71

The Grace to Be You

We are God's handiwork, created in Christ Jesus to do good works, which God prepared in advance for us to do.

—EPHESIANS 2:10

We've all done it at some point—looked at another person wishing we could have her looks, her career, her family, the list goes on. When this happens, we need to realize what is actually happening: the enemy is trying to get us discouraged and off track as he turns our eyes away from Jesus.

God created each one of us with a unique purpose that only we can fulfill. He equipped us with everything we need in order to do that good work, and He certainly does not make mistakes. When we live according to the plan He created for us, when we follow His guidance to fulfill the purpose He has for us, we will find that we have everything we need to do what He calls us to do. Why is it, then, that many of us get caught in a place in life where we feel stressed, tired, and worn out? This exhaustion and frustration may be the result of trying to be something we were never meant to be or to obtain something we were never meant to have.

When we are trying to operate outside of what God created us to be or to have, it won't be long before we find ourselves in a place of turmoil. This is a direct result of straining for things that are outside of God's gracious plan for our lives.

God has awesome plans for each one of us. When we stick to the plan that He created us for, we will find fulfillment, peace, and joy because we are operating in the grace that He gives us to live each day to the fullest, to live each day for Him.

> **Lord, I thank You** for creating me to fulfill the specific purpose that You have for me. Please help me keep my eyes focused on You as You lead me along that path. Help me know contentment in You as I operate in the grace You give me to live each day for You. In Jesus' name, amen.

If you have enjoyed this book
or it has touched your life in some way,
we would love to hear from you.

Please send your comments to:

Hallmark Book Feedback

P.O. Box 419034

Mail Drop 100

Kansas City, MO 64141

Or e-mail us at:

booknotes@hallmark.com